WILDLIFE
IN THE CITY

'All the summer long,' wrote Gilbert White two hundred years ago, 'is the swallow a most instructive pattern of unwearied industry and affection. from morning to night, while there is a family to be supported.'

WILDLIFE IN THE CITY

Animals, birds, reptiles, insects
and plants in an urban landscape

ALAN C. JENKINS

Webb&Bower

EXETER, ENGLAND

For Chipco

First published in Great Britain 1982 by
Webb & Bower (Publishers) Limited
9 Colleton Crescent, Exeter, Devon EX2 4BY

Designed by Vic Giolitto

Picture research by Anne-Marie Ehrlich

Text Copyright © Alan C. Jenkins 1982
Illustrations and Design Copyright © Webb & Bower (Publishers) Limited

British Library Cataloguing in Publication Data

Jenkins, Alan C.
  Wildlife in the city.
  1. Urban fauna
  2. Urban flora
  I. Title
  574.909′73′2   QH45.5
  ISBN 0-906671-56-6

Typeset in Great Britain by August Filmsetting Limited, Warrington, Cheshire

Printed and bound in Great Britain by Hazell Watson and Viney Limited, Aylesbury, Buckinghamshire

Contents

CHAPTER ONE

Man and Nature

In recent years much interest and attention has been paid to urban wildlife, as if it were a new phenomenon. But as the Book of Ecclesiastes has it, 'there is no new thing under the sun'. It is largely man who has invaded and despoiled the wild creatures' habitat, not the other way round.

It should be said at the outset that in the present context, 'city' has been used in its widest meaning, for originally the word meant any town or inhabited place. The scope of this book is certainly not confined to, let us say, the Premier Arrondissement, the bustling quarter that contains the Bourse and the erstwhile belly of Paris, Les Halles, or the square mile constituting that financial ant-heap, the City of London, or the overworked heart of New York round Wall Street or Madison Square. But to have talked in terms of 'Wildlife in Urban Areas, including suburbs, precincts, and outlying sections', might have been a little too cumbersome.

Accepting, then, city in this looser form, wildlife has always existed in it or *on* the site where it was ultimately built. Long before man came on the scene, let alone walked upright, the giant reptiles roamed the primaeval forests and swamps where now proud metropolises stand, where concert-halls resound to sublime music, expression of man's yearning to prove himself more than a brute beast, majestic council chambers where he attempts, all too vainly, to control his affairs, or vast enterprises that produce all the aids and comforts and contrivances to raise him, he thinks, far above the skin-clad existence he once followed.

Where London's St Paul's Cathedral now stands, the fearsome Tyrannosaurus once hunted the long-necked Diplodocus, defenceless in spite of its ninety-foot length. In Los Angeles huge numbers of fossil remains of prehistoric creatures have been found in the La Brea tar-pits—natural traps for unwary animals whose carcases were then fought over by such carrion-eaters as the Teratornis, ancestor of the condor, and one of the largest flying birds that ever existed, but whose wing-span of twelve feet didn't save it from the same fate in that implacable 'glue'.

Still farther on along the avenues of time came the mammoth and the cave-bear and the woolly rhinoceros, the musk-ox and the saiga antelope, all of whose remains have been found beneath the streets of London. Much later on again, when man had forsaken his nomadic existence, taken to

Perhaps as a symbol of human dominance of the earth, these New York buildings tower above Central Park. But the wild duck, too, are a symbol of nature's refusal to be ousted completely from the city.

Clearly these pied wagtails in Cork feel that the man-made city is merely incidental. All they seek is shelter and warmth. Winter flocks of this species sometimes number several hundred.

settled farming, and then eventually built the 'city', wildlife was still there. It was man who was the intruder, for he raised his settlements in the accustomed haunts of wild animals. It was only natural that to begin with the animals should try to stay put—not only was this their grazing, their hunting-ground, their nesting-scrub, but they had long been used to man and were probably far less afraid of him in those far-off days, for the simple reasons that his numbers were infinitely fewer and his weapons far less efficient. In the balance of nature the man with the bow and arrow weighed far less than the man with the gun.

In addition, the city was far 'greener', town and country were far less rigidly divided—even in mediaeval times in cities such as London or Paris, little farms and orchards were intermingled with the houses, pigs and poultry and geese roamed the streets which were largely open sewers. But as man became progressively more numerous and more demanding in his material needs, so he became increasingly intolerant of wild competition. For long the wild creatures did not appreciate this—they kept returning, rather like those nomadic Lapps of the last century who could not understand it when their age-old grazing lands were whittled away by the colonizing Finns in their seasonal absences. Nothing had ever been put down in legal jargon for the protection of the Lapps; even less so for the wild animals who tried to come back to or remain in the cities of the world!

Even in modern times wildlife still could not take in this usurpation of their natural territory. For example, in the case of New York, first settled by the Dutch, who had called it New Amsterdam, then by the English who acquired it in 1664 as a going concern of one thousand souls: from time immemorial the forests and reaches of the Hudson River and Manhattan had been the hunting-ground or feeding-place of bear and mountain lion and white-tailed deer and moose and wild turkey. Gradually, such wild creatures were either slaughtered by the ever-improving gun or forced out by ever-increasing human numbers, for habitat-destruction has been going on ever since mankind was exhorted to 'be fruitful and multiply'. Some wild species were more obstinate in their reluctance to be evicted from their natural haunts and it is ironical that in this respect the most obstinate was the wolf, probable ancestor of the domestic animal that has always been closest to man. As late as the 1770s, the decade that saw the American Revolution, the last British Governor of New York (which was by then a flourishing community of twenty thousand people) was obliged to publish a decree to the effect that

> because divers inhabitants of this colony have suffered many grievous losses in their stock, both of sheep and neat cattle, for prevention of which and encouragement of those who shall destroy wolves in the said colony, and that the breed of wolves within New York may be wholly rooted out and extinguished, be it enacted that there be paid twenty shillings for a grown wolf killed by a Christian, ten shillings for such a wolf killed by an Indian, and half that sum respectively for a whelp.

The discrepancy in the tariff is presumably simply a tribute to the greater tracking skill of the Redman.

But though 'big game', such as wolf and deer, were for varying reasons chased out or extirpated, much wildlife remained or took up residence in city areas, either because their winged character gave them an advantage or because they were so small they were overlooked or were too difficult to deal with or because they were useful to man—who is at his most tolerant when gaining some benefit. Chief among the wildlife in this category were the scavengers which, as we shall see, were (and still are in some cities of the world) of immense help to man, who is perhaps the filthiest creature in existence and seemingly incapable of properly controlling his habits. These scavengers comprise a large number of the natural species that have taken up residence in city and town. Nature is an opportunist, and many wild creatures have always appreciated that man, albeit unwittingly, provides food or shelter or both. Some such as kite and vulture have hung around mainly for the food; rat and mouse have gratefully accepted board *and* lodging. The fox, a newcomer to the urban scene, is an example of nature's adaptability, not only dwelling quite blatantly in the midst of human habitations, but turning scavenger as well.

There is another aspect of all this. In view of all that man has done to wildlife over the centuries—and particularly during our own century— it is an ironic fact that some species, even if they don't yet appreciate it, may well be more secure in the company of human-beings than in the open countryside where the farmer, for example, is not exactly the whole-hearted friend of wildlife conservation. In addition, the countryside every-where is shrinking—in Britain alone, an area equivalent to the county of Warwickshire is being swallowed up every decade by building and roads and factory sites. In the United States of America, environmentalists are preparing for what has been called the ecological battle of the century against the vanguard of free enterprise who are out to grab even the once-sacrosanct national parks.

So the fox that takes up residence on Bookham Common or Bristol Downs and raids the neighbourhood garbage-bins or the muskrat that colonizes the swampland of New York's Van Cortland Park may be safer than their rural counterparts. In Britain in one recent year 100,000 fox-skins found their way on to the market because of the high prices they fetch. But in town areas there is ostensibly no shooting, no hunting, no trapping, no large-scale spraying. The badgers that inhabit places such as Wimbledon Common or Richmond Park and even some suburban gardens (sometimes unknown to the owners) are safer than, say, in the West Country, where the Ministry of Agriculture gassing campaign*—a policy carried out by Britain alone among Western European countries— together with illegal and brutal badger-digging, could quite possibly turn a 'protected' species into an endangered one.

Unhappily the numbers of these urban animals are inevitably small in comparison. As much as a century ago in *Nature near London*, Richard Jefferies drew attention to this 'safety' aspect of wildlife in urban areas.

There are more crows round London than in a whole county, where the absence of manufactures and the rural quiet would seem favourable to bird life. The reason, of course, is that in the country the crows fre-quenting woods are shot and kept down as much as possible by game-keepers. In the immediate environs of London, keepers are not about, and even a little further away the land is held by many small owners, and game preservation is not thought of.

Gamekeepers, of course, are no longer so thick on the ground, but their depredations have been more than amplified by farming interests, in the

*Suspended, July 1982.

For the birds, city life is more feasible than for big mammals
such as these elk (mother and calf), or moose
as they are known in America. The city gates are
shut to these magnificent deer.

bulldozing of hedgerows—140,000 miles since 1945—the felling of woodland—one third of all the small woods in England and Wales in the same
period—the indiscriminate use of chemicals which have broken up so
many food-chains.

Supplementing the possibility that some species may be safer in urban
areas is man's changing attitude to nature. Once upon a time, for example,
it was the automatic practice to cut down every tree in sight round a new
housing estate. Nowadays, urban man, progressively cemented in, hankers
not only for refreshing greenery, but also for the company of wildlife, in
however insignificant a form. He welcomes the presence of squirrels in the
municipal park—the bird-table outside his kitchen gives him constant
pleasure—he exercises his powers of identification on the pinioned wildfowl on the recreation-pond—he is gladdened by the phalanxes of willow-
herb on some old bomb-site or building-plot—he is thrilled by a glimpse
of fox-cubs from his commuter-train—persuading mendacious pigeon or

Our forefathers would not have been particularly surprised at this picture of a cow wandering freely through an Indian street. Staying in the town of Chatham when he was Secretary to the Admiralty, Samuel Pepys complained of being 'wakened by a damned noise' made by cows and pigs.

house-sparrow or black-headed gull to come to hand is an adventure.

As far back as the 1890s, W. H. Hudson could see the essential value of urban parks and commons and small-scale wildernesses as sanctuaries for nature's refugees. 'Even on the borders of London,' he wrote in *Birds of London*, 'we have such places, and perhaps it would be hard anywhere in the rural districts to find a more perfect sanctuary in a small space than that of Caen Wood, at Hampstead. Although at the side of the swarming Heath, it is really wild, since for long years it has been free from the landscape gardener with his pretty little conventions, and the gamekeeper and henwife with their persecutions and playing at Providence among the creatures. If it were possible for a man to climb to the top of one of its noble old trees—a tall cedar, beech, or elm, with a girth of sixteen to eighteen feet—he would look down and out upon London: leagues upon leagues of houses, stretching away to the southern horizon, with tall chimneys, towers and spires innumerable appearing above the brooding cloud of smoke. But the wood itself seems not to have been touched by its sulphurous breath; within its green shade all is fresh as in any leafy retreat a hundred miles from town. And here the wild creatures find a refuge. Badgers—not a pair nor two, but a big colony—have their huge subterraneous peaceful village in the centre of the wood. The lodge-keeper's wife told me that one evening, seeing her dog, as she imagined, trotting from her across the lawn, she called to him and, angered at his disregard of her voice, ran after him for some distance among the trees, and only when she was about to lay her hands on him discovered that she was chasing a big badger. The badgers have for neighbours stoats and weasels and rabbits, carrion crows, jays and owls. Even in the daytime you will find the wood-owl dozing in the deep twilight of a holly-bush growing in the shade of a huge oak or elm. High up on the trees at least half a dozen pairs of carrion crows have their nests; and occasionally all the birds gather at one spot and fill the entire wood with their tremendous excited cries. A dozen of these birds, when they let themselves go, will create a greater uproar than a hundred cawing rooks. The moorhen and the wood-pigeon flourish, and in a still greater degree the missel-thrush, throstle and blackbird. In this wood I have counted forty-three species; and not only is the variety great, but many of our best songsters, residents and migrants, are so numerous that at certain times in spring, when birds are most vocal, you may hear at this spot as fine a concert of sweet voices as in any wood in England.' And Hudson went on to say, 'it should be our aim to have all the parks, even to the most central, as nearly like sanctuaries as such small isolated urban species, inhabited by so limited a number of species, may be made.'

He wrote that nearly eighty-five years ago. Today, every urban open space, every city park, every track of commonland, every neighbourhood pond, even the abandoned cemetery, even the wasteland round the local rubbish-dump, becomes increasingly precious and important, supporting

In places, remnants of the past linger on, when countryside and city merged one with another, as in this pastoral scene at Kenwood on the edge of London.

as they do an entire ecology of their own, fox, kestrel, field-vole, redstart, red admiral and many, many other species that would astonish and gratify the townsman. If the steady increase of human numbers is inevitable, the accompanying urban sprawl could at least be mitigated by leaving more and more oases in its midst as small scale refuges for the creatures of the wild.

All over the world even once inviolate wildlife reserves are threatened by human demands. The elephant in Africa and the tiger in India are probably doomed. Is it possible that the gloomy words of E. P. Gee will come true: 'Imagine the year 2000, with the only wild life consisting of those creatures which can adapt themselves easily to thickly populated areas, such as jackals, rats, mice, vultures, pariah and Brahminy kites, crows and sparrows!'

CHAPTER TWO

Wild Familiars

Probably the wildlife best known to townspeople world-wide is a trio of birds—the house-sparrow, feral pigeon, and starling. From New York to Peking, they are by far the commonest avian residents, sharing an appreciation of human bounty and resisting all efforts to control them.

The most notorious, most numerous, and most adaptable, is the house-sparrow, not a member of the finch family as some people think, nor a relation of the dunnock which is frequently slandered by being dubbed the hedge-sparrow. The house-sparrow is as universal as the rat, flourishing in habitats as varied as the sub-arctic towns of Sweden and the tropical cities of Brazil. But as a pillager it is not in the same league. All the same, it has always aroused mixed emotions. Thus the condemnation published a century ago in a horticultural journal in Australia, where the species had been introduced (by similar well-meaning nature-lovers as those who introduced the rabbit with disastrous results)—

> We can't defeat a foe like this
> With gunshot or with bows and arrows;
> We must resort to artifice
> To cope with enemies like sparrows—

which conflicts with the sentiment of a townsman in America where the species had been introduced at the same time. 'I imagine no Yankee would wish now to be without the life and animation of the house sparrow in his great cities. They are like gaslight in a town—a sign of progress. I admit the bird is a little blackguard—fond of low society and full of fight, stealing and love-making—but he is death on insects, fond of citizen life, and in every way suited to be an inhabitant of the New World.'

A series of releases was made between the years 1850 and 1870 in places such as Brooklyn, Rhode Island, Pennsylvania, Ohio. The sparrow seized joyfully on this man-given opportunity and its numbers in America exploded like some feathered *feu d'artifice*, for, astonishingly, it was for long a protected bird. The American naturalist W. B. Burrows summed up the situation in the United States when, writing in 1889, he said

> The marvellous rapidity of the sparrow's multiplication, the surpassing swiftness of its extension, and the prodigious size of the area it has overspread are without parallel in the history of any bird. Like a

This crowded scene in London gives an idea of how a whole ecology was radically changed with the disappearance of horse transport. Birds, small mammals, insects were all affected. Petrol feeds nobody, only poisons us.

noxious weed transplanted to a fertile soil, it has taken root and become disseminated over half a continent before the significance of its presence has come to be understood. It has completely overrun the country.

But the city with which the house-sparrow has always been most closely identified is London, the attitude of whose people was typified by Hudson's two workmen, 'big, strong men, with tired, dusty faces', who regularly on their way home from work 'produced from their coat-pockets a little store of bread and meat saved from their midday meal, carefully wrapped in a piece of newspaper. After bestowing their scraps on the little brown-coated crowd of sparrows, one would say: "Come on, mate, they've had it all, so now let's go home and see what the missus has got for *our* tea"; and home they would trudge across Hyde Park with hearts refreshed and lightened.'

Any day in the London parks the same scene is re-enacted, with house-

Town starlings are regular scavengers. But in North African countries enormous migrant flocks sometimes ruin date palms and olive groves.

sparrows coming to hand and even perching on the shoulders and arms of their human benefactors. And of course they long ago twigged what a profitable hunting-ground is the zoo in Regent's Park. It is a nice contrast to watch them prospecting under the drowsy eyes of lion or tiger.

Though they have been described as 'vulgar little birds, too common to need description', these house-sparrows do bring a touch if not precisely of wildlife at least a droll reminder of the whole world of nature to which we belong. Though the Londoner might wonder at other more exotic and colourful species that appear from time to time—the red-backed shrike that has occasionally nested close by the North Circular Road or the nightingale which, if not in Berkeley Square, has sung on Wimbledon Common—his attitude to the sparrow—Philip, from time immemorial—is one of sympathetic, amused affection. He likes its cockney impudence and cheerfulness, its everlasting prattle, pip pip, churrup churrup or whatever. He admires its sober handsomeness—in which it is rather like some impecunious person who puts on worn but respectable garb—and, if you make allowance for city discoloration, the sparrow is truly handsome, with its chestnut mantle, grey crown and rump, black chin and throat. (The chief means of differentiating between the house-sparrow and the rarer tree-sparrow is the chestnut head and cheek patches of the latter.)

Above all, the townsman appreciates the sparrow's sociableness—not only for mankind but towards its fellows. The lone swan—the lone swallow —the lone curlew, maybe—but never the lone sparrow. Like many human-beings he can't abide being alone and he will colonize just anywhere—ivy-clad walls, chimney-stacks, factory roofs, house-martins' nests —at the Great Exhibition of 1851 sparrows caused such a nuisance by immediately and gleefully setting up shop in that gigantic glass-house it was suggested that sparrow-hawks should be brought in to deal with them.

In his matiness the house-sparrow reminds one of his close relation, the sociable weaver-bird of southern Africa, a couple of hundred pairs of which will band together to make an enormous communal nest like some avian tower-block. But sociable though the house-sparrow is he is not above pulling a fast one on his neighbour. Howard Lancum once told of two house-sparrows' nests that were being built in a suburban garden. 'The pair of birds responsible for the nearer nest have come upon a labour-saving discovery of some consequence, which is that a mass of ready-to-hand material, all in one place, is better than a mass that has to be collected piecemeal from here, there and everywhere. Most regrettably, the ready-to-hand material in this case is the partly built nest of the other pair of sparrows, who, if they are as intelligent as sparrows generally appear to be, must be sorely puzzled by the slowness of their own progress. This sinful game has been played for some days, and it is surprising that the victims have not yet realized what is going on, although it is true that the repeated thefts are carried out with circumspection and a cunning remarkable even in house-sparrows. But it seems inevitable that, sooner or later, one of the robbers must be caught red-handed, and when that happens there will certainly be trouble.'

But if 'it's being so cheerful that keeps me going' could be taken as the spiritual motto of the house-sparrow, in a material sense it is being a commensal of man that sustains it. Rarely does the species establish itself away from the company of human-beings. It has been scientifically estimated that each house-sparrow consumes up to eight pounds of food every year, most of it grain, while as the sparrow population in Britain alone has been calculated at nearly ten million, an interesting sum could be worked out, though the sparrow's numbers have fallen considerably with the disappearance of horse-drawn traffic, while modern buildings provide far fewer nesting sites. Various means of off-setting its depredations have been tried out, from poisoning by 'Faulding's Phoenix wheat' advocated by that Australian gardener mentioned earlier, to the age-old habit of some

Judging by the onlookers in this drawing from the *Illustrated London News* of 1877, feeding the birds was more of a novelty than nowadays.

European peasants when sowing, of flinging the first handful of seed backwards over their heads while saying 'Sparrows, that is for you, please leave the rest alone!' And in modern China, a few years ago, when a plague of sparrows threatened the harvest, a nation-wide campaign was organized, in which in hundreds of towns and villages men, women and children were mustered to maintain a ceaseless cacophony by beating trays and utensils so that the wretched birds could not even settle to roost, let alone feed, eventually falling to the ground in large numbers, to die through sheer exhaustion or be destroyed.

In Britain in the past, a partial solution was to *eat* the sparrows—the poor man's ortolan, perhaps. Sparrow-clubs existed in many parts of the country and sparrow-pie was greatly esteemed. A regular tariff was paid, tuppence or threepence a dozen being fairly normal. The idea even caught on for a while in New Zealand—which the bird had extensively colonized after being introduced in 1866, originally to combat swarms of caterpillars —but it doesn't seem to have had much effect on the sparrow population. We have, by various means, contrived to destroy many beautiful creatures, from cheetah to goshawk, from otter to tiger, and so on, but we never seem able to control the real 'pests'—as we term them in our subjective way.

But pest, scavenger, parasite, whatever you like to call the house-sparrow, probably no other bird except the robin has enjoyed a more prominent place in literature—from the biblical promise that a sparrow 'shall not fall on the ground without your Father's knowledge' to Shakespeare's echo of that, 'there's a special providence in the fall of a sparrow', or from John Skelton's fifteenth-century *Book of Philip Sparrow* to Clare Kipps's much translated *Sold for a Farthing*, while portrayals of the sparrow have varied from the caddish murderer of Cock Robin in the age-old nursery rhyme to the anonymous poet's eulogy—

> Of all the birds that I do know,
>   Philip my sparrow hath no peer;
> For sit she high, or sit she low,
>   Be she far off, or be she near,
> There is no bird so fair, so fine,
> Nor yet so fresh as this of mine;
> For when she once hath felt a fit,
> Philip will cry still: *Yet, yet, yet.*

Besides, what other bird has achieved such immortality as to be stuffed and mounted on a cricket ball in the headquarters of the MCC at Lord's, where, on a fateful day half a century ago, it was literally bowled out by one Jehangir Khan of Cambridge University. That, surely, is the cue for the entrance of another poet, the seventeenth-century William Cartwright:

> Tell me not of joy: there's none,
> Now my little Sparrow's gone,

a sentiment that would certainly be echoed by a tough French sea-captain I once knew who wept when his pet sparrow escaped from its cage and was eaten by his cat.

As for the pigeon, its relationship with man is much longer and closer than that of the house-sparrow. For man has exploited it in one way or another for countless centuries. He elevated the 'dove' into a symbol of love and peace, but at the same time ate the birds with great relish—from which possibly there is a certain Freudian inference to be drawn. The Ancient Egyptians used it to carry messages, having readily appreciated the bird's homing instincts. The Romans fattened it for the table, keeping the birds in special *columbaria*, forerunner of the dovecot, where they were force-fed after having their wings clipped or legs broken to prevent their escape. Even during the Second World War, more than two hundred thousand pigeons were used by British military authorities, including many thousands that were parachuted for the use of Resistance movements. Some pigeons even carried miniature cameras over war-zones.

Many different kinds of pigeon exist or existed, members of the family Columbidae being found variously all over the world except in the polar regions. Some have achieved fame in an unfortunate way. The dodo, of a different family, the Raphidae, but of the same order Columbiformes, suffered from three drawbacks. It was as big as a swan, equally edible, and could not fly. So during the early seventeenth century, when international commerce was booming, it fell victim to meat-hungry sailors who butchered it on its native island of Mauritius, its memory being perpetuated in the saying 'dead as a dodo'. The solitaire, that other large, wingless relation of the pigeon, went the same way.

Ill-famed indeed was an American member of the pigeon family. This was the lovely passenger pigeon, grey with red lustres and varying shades of blue. Audubon, who painted the bird with his customary flair, gave a dramatic account of a migrating flock that he watched near Louisville in 1813. He was so staggered that he guessed wildly at a figure of more than a thousand million—the feathered multitude darkened the sky—and when the flocks roosted, branches broke under their weight. Another observer spoke of a compact flying mass of pigeons at least five miles long on a front one mile wide and that later a stretch of woodland twenty-eight miles long was taken up by nesting birds, every tree of any size having some nests, others being filled with them.

Subsequently, yet again, man ran amok, the passenger pigeon was ruthlessly shot or netted, thousands of barrels of salted pigeon meat were shipped every year, and by 1914 the last survivor of the species, 'Martha', had died in Cincinnati Zoo.

Nowadays, many members of the pigeon family remain, varying from the largest species—considerably larger than a pheasant—the Victoria crowned pigeon of New Guinea, with its elaborate head-dress, to the peaceful-dove of Australia, the size of a song-thrush. In municipal areas of America and Canada, the beautiful mourning-dove often nests in garden shrubberies, even scavenges among the barnyard hens. In town areas of Britain and Europe, the legendary voice of the turtle-dove can sometimes be heard. The stock-dove nests regularly in parks and on commons. Often to be seen is the ecstatic nuptial display flight of the ring-dove or wood-pigeon as it rises at a steep angle and then glides down with scarcely open wings. And in recent years the collared dove, spreading in remarkable fashion out of Asia Minor and across Europe, has become an established commensal of man—having started its city career in Istanbul.

But the 'real' bird of the city street is the feral pigeon. This is descended from the rock-dove, *Columba livia*, whose natural haunts could scarcely be in greater contrast with the tarmac and concrete habitat of the all too familiar town bird. On the north-western coasts of the British Isles it nests among the sea-thrift of Atlantic cliffs or in the dusky caves that bring an echo of Mendelssohn's music, its companions, guillemots and razorbills

Kenwood House, whose elegant grounds form a natural haven for many wild creatures within sight and sound of London's tumultuous streets.

Buddleia, wormwood, hoary mustard, scentless mayweed, London rocket, are among the wild flowers springing from a base of rubble at the William Curtis Ecological Park in London.

Central Park offers the New Yorker a flimsy but welcome touch of nature,
remote for a moment from the city's fevered round. As Robert Frost wrote, 'keep
us here / All simply in the springing of the year.'

and kittiwakes and the comical puffins with their gaudy, striped, parrot bills, standing outside their rabbit-burrow homes like portly little shop-keepers clad in white aprons. In India the rock-dove haunts the ruined fortresses of the Moghuls, refuges of snake and scorpion. In North Africa its home is high above the glittering Mediterranean, among the cedars and junipers of the lower Atlas slopes.

But the street-pigeon itself, which is equally at home among the milling tourists gazing at the Doge's Palace in Venice or city workers to-ing and fro-ing in Times Square, is not the result of the wild 'blue' rock-dove changing its habitat and taking up residence in the city as with, say, the starling or various gulls. The hordes of feral pigeons in towns from Bangkok to Berlin originated from domesticated birds escaped from dovecots or from racing pigeons that had strayed or become lost. Man of course captured and bred the rock-dove for food long before he took up the hobby of racing the bird. Those in authority enjoyed a virtual monopoly of the pigeon in mediaeval times, nobles and prelates and lords of the manor building elaborate dovecots, some of them extremely handsome and spacious in the design, and their occupants fed largely on the grain grown by peasants and yeoman.

The dovecot and the dove became symbols not of peace but of hatred among the lower orders. 'Most of all,' wrote G. M. Trevelyan, 'did it rejoice the farmer's heart to slay secretly for his own pot one of the legion of privileged birds from the dovecot of the manor-house whose function in life was to grow plump on the peasant's corn till they were fit for the table.' In the fifteenth century the Fellows of King's College, Cambridge, ate or sold three thousand doves a year from the great dovecot of their Grant-chester estate.

Escapes from dovecots were happening all the time and the city population of feral pigeons increased progressively. Even in the fourteenth century the Bishop of London warned that much damage was done in St Paul's Cathedral by people trying to dislodge or destroy nesting birds. Samuel Pepys in his famous diary records that during the Great Fire of London in 1666 (which destroyed 13,000 houses and eighty churches) 'the poor pigeons, I perceive, were loth to leave the houses and hovered about the windows and balconys till their wings were burned and they fell down'.

But it was during the last century that the feral pigeon as a city dweller began to increase remarkably, large colonies being reported on buildings such as the British Museum and the Houses of Parliament. By the 1960s feral pigeons had become more numerous than sparrows by an estimated fifty per cent. In the very heart of London, in an area ten square miles round Charing Cross, there were perhaps fifty thousand pigeons, one of their favourite pads being Trafalgar Square. The same thing was happening in the United States, to which the pigeon had first been introduced by

But in our concrete world, contact with nature becomes
ever more precious to the townsman.

These pigeons have found a comfortable bench in the park—Grosvenor Square, to be exact—perhaps while they await the arrival of one of their local human benefactors.

the settlers of the seventeenth century. Nowadays it has become the most familiar bird of American cities.

As with the wood-pigeon and stock-dove, the diet of the rock-dove was grain and berries and greenstuffs, but the city bird has become virtually omnivorous, being quite prepared to add fruit and worms and bread and insects and meat and fish to its menu, and always ready to plunder bird-tables in suburban gardens. But in addition to the advantages it enjoys as a commensal of man, it finds ideal nesting sites on city skyscrapers and tower-blocks and bridges and parapets and church-steeples—what could better resemble those far-off rocky ledges and beetling crevices than the man-sards and drain-hoppers and pilasters and roofs, especially as the species builds the flimsiest of nests: none of your intricate work for the pigeon such as the devoted thrush or chaffinch goes in for.

Once a favourable site is settled on by a flock of feral pigeons (for they still tend to keep in tight-knit groups), generation after generation of birds will go on nesting in the same place. A few years ago a gruesome example of this was discovered by demolition workers in the attic of a long-derelict courthouse in Greenwich Village in New York. The room was littered deeply with the remains of dead birds, the live pigeons not bothering to make any nests but simply laying their eggs on the sordid heaps of feathers and bones and decomposing carcasses, while newly hatched squabs jostled with fledglings trying out their wings.

This sort of instance illustrates why the feral pigeon is anathema to city and town authorities all over the world. They stress the health hazards, for pigeons are potential carriers of bacteria and viruses to which human-beings are susceptible. They accuse the birds of attacking the mortar of buildings, which is undoubtedly so, as the pigeons are seeking lime. Pigeons also foul up buildings to a great extent—in one clean-up of the Foreign Office in London, fifty tons of droppings and nesting material were removed from the roof and ledges. Many methods of controlling the huge numbers of pigeons have been tried out—shooting, catapult netting, mist-spraying with ammonia, all have proved inadequate. Grain has been treated with alpha-chloralose which so stupefies the birds that they are afterwards easy to catch and destroy, a method adopted in various muni-cipalities of America, Australia, France, Germany and Sweden.

But the most bizarre attempt at reducing, or even limiting the feral pigeon population has been by contraceptive methods. In the American town of Bangor, in Maine, the chemical 'ornitrol' was said to have worked to some extent, while in Venice the contraceptive pill was included among the grain fed to the pigeons in St Mark's Square. The birds accepted the pills greedily enough but there has been no falling off in their numbers as a result. (Perhaps Venice should study Pisa's efforts with their rats—see below.)

However, apart from the occasional hazard of being 'dropped on', most city folk probably enjoy the presence of the pigeon, and indeed are largely responsible for its numbers, encouraging it by the vast quantities of food such as bread that are put out for it or fed to it in park and square. And in this respect it is interesting that in some English towns, for instance, when bread was rationed during wartime years, the pigeon population is said to have fallen off. Even more than the sparrow, say, the pigeon repres-ents the wild come to the city, in addition to which ordinary people still retain that image of the 'dove' as a sign of peace and hope—witness the ritual release of birds at any Olympic Games. Moreover, the flight of the pigeon has always evoked our admiration—from the sudden explosion of wings as a flock rises like the opening of some huge surrealist flower, to the thrilling speed of the pigeon in full flight, and speed the pigeon assuredly needed in the wild to elude its chief predators, goshawk and peregrine: even in some cities there have been instances of attacks by such raptors.

'O that I had wings like a dove!' yearned the psalmist, 'for then could I fly away, and be at rest.' And unconsciously perhaps the city dweller echoes this sentiment and is happy to see the hundreds of pigeons that attend him as he threads his way each morning among the towering chasms of the city where the roar of traffic does proxy for the surging waves that beat against the wild rock-dove's haunts.

The third member of the trio, the starling, is not known so intimately to the townsman. In London, for example, it is in large part a commuter, roosting in its tens of thousands on city buildings and flying sometimes nearly twenty miles out to feed each morning, before once again returning to make the window ledges and eaves resound with its sibilant bickering and chattering as it settles down for the night, undisturbed by the neon blaze around it. Similarly, in cities such as Glasgow, enormous roosts of perhaps fifty thousand birds come and go daily, their numbers nationwide augmented in winter by millions of starlings from mainland Europe. The massed flight of migrating starlings sounds like the rustle of the sea.

Yet the starling as a city or urban commuter is a fairly recent phenomenon. It is barely one hundred years ago since the fact of a pair of birds nesting in Richmond Park was worthy of note in *The Field* magazine, while the bird was first mentioned as roosting in Inner London in a letter to *The Times* in 1894. But in general the species was evidently well enough known in mediaeval times, for in the fifteenth-century *Boke of St Albans*, Dame Berners refers to 'a murmuracion of stares'.

As for the United States, after various well-intentioned but unsuccessful attempts, one hundred starlings were released in Central Park, New York, in 1890–91. The proverbial 'duck to water' had nothing on those starlings. Half a century later, the starling population of America was estimated at fifty million, about one per cent of the entire avian population of the United States and the species had even arrived in Alaska. It is said that at times flocks of 100,000 starlings roost on bridges over the Raritan River in New Jersey.

The spread of the starling, both in general and as a bird of city and town, has been phenomenal and world-wide—and largely through human agency, as in the case of the house-sparrow. It was introduced into Cape Town, in South Africa, reputedly by Cecil Rhodes, and rapidly extended its range. From thirty-six birds released in Victoria, Australia, in 1863, the starling has now firmly established itself in much of the country (the Northern Territory and Western Australia being exceptions), including the major cities such as Sydney and Melbourne, and has by its competition adversely affected the native bird population. Similarly, at about the same time, well-meaning nature-lovers introduced seventeen starlings into New Zealand, where the species is now a familiar resident in Wellington and Dunedin, for example. Here again, native birds have been radically affected through the starling's aggressive occupation of nesting sites and single-mindedness over food. You have only to watch a mob of starlings on

An illustration from William Yarrell's *History of British Birds* (1845). Only the artist could say to a certainty what manner of bird looks down enviously from its cage at the pouter and fantail pigeons strutting in liberty.

your bird-table to appreciate their excellent time-and-motion methods.

Agriculturally, the starling is a controversial bird. Undoubtedly those enormous flocks do great damage to crops and fruit. On the other hand they also destroy untold numbers of 'noxious' insects such as chafer and cranefly grubs, while in America sixty years ago starlings were largely responsible for checking the swarms of the accidently imported Japanese beetle that was ravaging the land.

But as far as cities and towns are concerned, it is starling roosts that create the problem—and an established starling roost of any size is among the less pleasant phenomena in nature, or shall we say the results are. 'I counted two and seventy stenches, all well defined and several stinks,' wrote Coleridge in Cologne. We don't know for sure whether a starling roost was among his catalogue!

All sorts of methods of shifting the birds have been tried out, from sulphur flares and rockets to stuffed owls and even supersonic sound waves. Some of the devices are totally ignored by the starlings; others succeed briefly or merely cause the flocks to shift to another roost.

Leaving aside all its faults, there is no doubt that the starling at its best is a really beautiful bird. This is perhaps not as immediately apparent as in the case of such avian beauties as red cardinal or blue jay to be seen in American town parks and gardens or the bullfinches and goldfinches that frequent various English commons, but seen close-to the starling's spangled glossy plumage of shimmering, metallic purple, green and bronze is splendid indeed. Added to this is the bird's astonishing power of mimicry. It will sit on a chimney-pot, throat swelling raggedly, wings shivering as if it yearned to sing properly, and give a perfect rendering of other species as varied as green woodpecker, song-thrush, buzzard, curlew and many others.

In this attitude the starling resembles its close cousins, the mynas, familiar and handsome residents of many Indian towns. They chatter interminably in railway station and market, and many are kept as cage-birds in European countries, learning to 'talk' after a fashion, though the suburban drawing-room or lounge is more likely to echo with their sharp whistling and scolding cries than with any enlightening conversation.

Earlier, instead of referring to a *trio* of birds grown so familiar to townsfolk, we should have said quintet. For to house-sparrow and feral pigeon and starling must be added a couple of seagulls which in large numbers have radically changed their habits, becoming established town-dwellers.

In America the herring gull was once purely a bird of the wild Atlantic coast, its yelping 'kee-yow' or raucously defiant 'gah-gah-gah' echoing in counterpoint to the waves. But over the past half century it has become one of the commonest urban birds, frequenting city garbage dumps and reservoirs and parks and golf courses in considerable flocks. From being a pearly winged symbol of the sea-girt cliffs and rustling shores it has become a persistent commensal of man.

Likewise with the black-headed gull in Britain and north-west Europe. This pretty bird, scarcely bigger than a stock-dove, with its red bill and red legs and eponymous black or chocolate-brown nape (which to the confusion of some people fades to white in winter) has become a regular town-dweller. It nests regularly near some sewage-farms, notably at one time Perry Farm, close to London Airport, while one of its favourite haunts is St James's Park where it spends the winter, positively begging from human visitors with all the familiarity and boldness of any other wild scavenger.

It seems that a succession of severe winters may have led to black-headed gulls moving into urban areas, especially in the case of London, and in this connection we have a nice glimpse of how welcome any wild life is to the townsman. As Hudson said, 'Gulls came up the river Thames in greater force than ever and it was then that the custom of regularly feeding the gulls in London had its beginning. Every day for a period of three to four weeks hundreds of working men and boys would take advantage of the

These are tree-sparrows. The affection for sparrows in general is ageless. More than two thousand years ago the Roman poet Catullus wrote, 'My mistress's sparrow is dead, my mistress's pet which she loved more than her very eyes.'

free hour at dinner time to visit the bridges and embankments, and give the scraps left from their meals to the birds. The sight of this midday crowd hurrying down to the waterside with welcome in their faces and food in their hands must have come as "an absolute revelation" to the gulls.'

Certainly future generations of the species adopted London as their home town.

In recent years two other gulls have been observed at the garbage-dumps of both metropolitan London and New York. Perhaps the glaucous gull, alias the Burgomaster, largest of the species with a wing-span of at least five feet, picked up its scavenging habits in the past at whaling stations. As for the winter-wandering Iceland gull, it is almost identical in appearance with its imposing cousin except for its much smaller size. In proportion it is as the lesser black-backed gull is to the greater.

In general, the kites and ravens of long ago have been supplanted as urban rag-pickers by the gulls, whose pearly, luminous, soaring, majestic wings are more redolent of freedom and the ocean than of stinking, rat-infested masses of human ordures.

CHAPTER THREE
House-party

From the moment man built the first 'house', nature moved in. Many birds found ideal nesting space. Some animals found shelter too but at the same time helped people keep their homes free of parasites. Unknown to their human occupants many town dwellings contain an extensive natural history.

M y first night in India was beset by sleeplessness—not surprising amid all the cacophony of an oriental city—Cochin, to be exact. The clamour of human activity never ceased—merely changed character somewhat, not even abated—indeed, in some cases it rose to an even greater pitch in the velvety darkness studded with the drama of fireflies whose strange silvery light came and went as if at the touch of a switch. The greatest and most stirring uproar was caused by a Malayalam wedding party not far away, where a Kathakali dance was being performed by dancers in fearsome masks and gorgeous dresses, accompanied by the never-ending beat of drums and those inimitable high-pitched songs.

But nearer at hand was a more mysterious, more sinister noise—it came from overhead, from just above the ceiling of my bedroom. A swift, lunging slithering, then a bumping and knocking—the slithering sound faded— then suddenly came back more violently—and seemed closer than ever to my uneasy head. It didn't sound nice at all.

An explanation was forthcoming next morning.

'I hope our resident rat-catcher didn't keep you awake,' my host said at breakfast. 'He was particularly active last night. A lot more rats in the bungalow since last monsoon and he's really earning his keep.'

That particular rat-catcher was a snake, a six-foot 'rat-snake', a member of the Zamenis family, and a most effective rodent officer, welcome in households in much of India, though rarely as big as the individual in question. Dull brown in colour, with a yellowish belly, they keep very much to themselves and are gladly allowed the run of the loft or the outbuildings where they certainly earn their keep through the number of rodents they catch. Non-poisonous, but best left alone, my host said; can turn nasty if startled or cornered—and who wouldn't! Snake-charmers often use a rat-snake as part of the act, staging 'encounters' with their pet cobra—after sewing up the jaws of the much bigger rat-snake—the assumption being that the cobra has probably had its poison fangs removed.

That, however, is by the way.

Other welcome animals in that particular household, and Indian houses in general, were the geckos. These plump, thickset, rather big-

Geckos have sometimes been trained to come regularly to a dining-table and
accept the crumbs offered to them.

World-wide, some three hundred species of gecko exist. Some will often feed
together at night, but each has its own private sleeping-place
where it spends the day.

headed, nocturnal lizards are immensely useful because of the numbers of insects they catch. They are best known for two characteristics—a kind of muscular suction pad on the underside of their disc-like, prominent toes enables them not only to scurry up and down the walls of a room but upside down across the ceiling, always a fascinating performance. And they are the only reptiles with a true voice (odd when you consider that the birds evolved from reptilian ancestors)—the largest of the family, the great house gecko, announces his arrival with something like a cackle, and then goes on interminably saying 'tok-i, tok-i, tok, tok', all night long.

In eastern towns the gecko is looked upon affectionately, not only for its useful work, but in Bangkok, for instance, it is reckoned an especially good sign if a gecko happens to be uttering its cry when a baby is born. In contrast, in Egyptian towns the lobe-footed gecko used to be regarded with dread, its vernacular name meaning 'father of leprosy'. In southern French and Spanish towns you can sometimes see the common or 'Moorish' gecko—for it emerges in daytime as well as by night, unlike the other purely nocturnal geckos. But it, too, is regarded with dread; to touch it was believed to cause instant death, and if you find it in your house it must at all costs be pursued and destroyed. Another of these insect-catching home-helps which often takes up residence in southern houses is the so-called Turkish gecko, barely three inches in length but with the peculiarity that its body wall is so thin the eggs can be seen through the skin of the female.

But the increasing use of insecticides, together with the pollution caused by motor-traffic in towns, has lessened the work, and diminished the livelihood, of such 'house-guests', as it has also done in the case of birds such as swallows and house-martins and swifts. Presumably such birds, especially the swallow-family, began their association with men in nomadic times, appreciating the swarms of insects that pestered the wandering herds. When men turned to a settled existence there was an added bonus in the shape of dwellings and shelters, primitive though these were, providing useful nesting sites—and a food-supply on the spot.

Even in those early days men wondered at the seasonal appearance and disappearance of such birds. Unable to account for this, they indulged in all manner of fantastic explanations, from the idea that they spent the winter in the upper air to the alternative that they rolled themselves *en masse* in the mud. It seems odd to us that it is less than two hundred years since the theory of bird-migration was generally accepted. Controversy raged over it for generations. In the seventeenth century, the great John Ray was quite certain that swallows migrated to Egypt or Ethiopia and he ridiculed the idea that they 'lurk in hollow trees or holes in the rocks or lie in water under the ice'. Yet his contemporary, Charles Morton, wrote an *Essay towards the Probable Solution of this question*—firmly believing that swallows and other birds migrated from the moon.

The omniscient Linnaeus believed that swallows hibernated; Gilbert

House-martins know all about solar energy. These birds are sunning themselves before migrating. They will need all their strength for a journey of several thousands of miles.

White wasn't at all certain. Yet already fifty years before him, the journalist Daniel Defoe had written in his *A Tour through England and Wales* (1724–6) that in the Suffolk town of Southwold he had one evening observed early in October

> an unusual multitude of birds sitting on the leads of the church; curiosity led me to go nearer to see what they were, and I found they were all swallows; that there was such an infinite number that they covered the whole roof of the church, and of several houses near; this led me to enquire of a grave gentleman whom I saw near me, what the meaning was of such a prodigious multitude of swallows sitting there; O sir, says he, turning towards the sea, you may see the reason, the wind is off the sea. I did not seem fully informed by that expression; so he goes on: I perceive, sir, says he, you are a stranger to it; you must then understand first that this is the season of the year when the swallows, their food here failing, begin to leave us, and return to the country, wherever it may be, from whence I suppose they came . . .

And next morning, Defoe records, every single one of the swallows, of which he reckoned there had been a 'million', had all vanished. But the reason for this strange phenomenon, he said, 'we must leave to the naturalists to determine, who insist upon it that brutes cannot think'.

Even today, however, the naturalists haven't unravelled all the mystery. We know that during their journeys across the world birds are helped by certain geographical features such as rivers, valleys, coastlines. But that doesn't account for the young of certain species finding their way long after their parents have departed. So how is it done? We are still not certain. We have to take refuge in the generalization that birds must possess some sort of in-built navigation kit, of which the most important part is an ability to take into consideration, first, the time of day, second, to make allowance for the position of sun or stars. Just as a human navigator in ship or aircraft does.

To most people sand-martins are not as familiar as house-martins or swallows. But migrating flocks sometimes gather in large numbers. Three thousand were recorded at Slapton Ley in Devon on one occasion in recent years.

Our knowledge of bird migration has perhaps advanced from the early 1600s, when the Bishop of Hereford, in his thesis *The Man in the Moone, A Discourse of a Voyage thither by Domingo Gonsales* put forward the idea of space travel by means of a flying-machine towed by migrating birds; nevertheless bird migration is for us still one of the many wonders of nature, while for the town-dweller especially, nothing is more cheering than the arrival of the first swallow or house-martin. For though in London such birds are mainly to be glimpsed in 'purlieus' such as Richmond Park, there are still provincial towns lucky enough to receive them, albeit, alas, in ever-decreasing numbers. In America the same 'barn' swallow still occasionally breeds on the northern outskirts of New York, far up the Hudson River, while for long the purple martin has nested on Staten Island in the Borough of Richmond.

In Britain, by the time the swifts arrive, the swallows (their exquisite small song probably unheard above the traffic) are already building or repairing their nests of grass and feathers, while the house-martins are industriously fetching pellets of mud, tirelessly again and again, to patch up their own superb little homes against the walls of the human dwellings they favour. Quite apart from insecticides and pollution, lack of mud is another handicap the martins suffer from in these days of tarmac. Where they are lucky enough to find any, they will queue up to take their tiny loads.

As for house-sparrows, not only do they default on the rent, but they cheekily invade the martins' nests at times and frequent squabbles take place. On this account Gilbert White called sparrows 'fell adversaries' of the martins, but he also pointed out that swifts often usurp the nests of house-sparrows which were 'up in arms, and much-disconcerted at these intruders'.

Once the swifts arrive, their shrill screaming and their hectic flight on those glorious scimitar wings that span perhaps fifteen inches are in ironic contrast with the earth-bound human activities below. We have to be thankful for any animal life in the town—anywhere at all, for that matter—but for me one of the most thrilling examples of this is a gang of swifts, scores together at times, racing in mad enjoyment—there's no other word for it—round and round some church or cathedral—for their favourite nesting places are in steeples and towers. And then, presently mounting higher and higher into the summer sky, until they are mere eyelashes, specks, fancies, and finally they vanish altogether, to spend the entire night on the wing.

All that is more likely in some southern town of France or Spain or Italy (and Indian towns, for that matter), whereas in London, only isolated cases of swifts nesting have been recorded in recent years at Kilburn and St John's Wood, while fifty years ago three pairs of swifts were recorded as nesting under the eaves of the General Post Office in the

37

heart of the city, the only breeding record since the days of Gilbert White, who presented a monograph on swifts to the Royal Society. 'In London a party of swifts frequents the Tower, playing and feeding over the river just below the bridge: others haunt some of the churches of the Borough next the fields; but do not venture, like the house-martin, into the close crowded part of the town.'

Yet swifts pay a generous rent wherever they live. The ornithologist David Lack showed that a pair of birds could take up to 20,000 insects a day!

As welcome in many European towns—in Germany, for example, where it is indeed the 'national' bird—is the white stork, which comes every spring from Africa. But its numbers have diminished even more than those of other visitors. Nevertheless, this grand bird, three and a half feet tall, with wings that span well over five feet, its glossy black and white plumage, its long red bill and red legs, still returns year after year to its favourite chimney-stacks and roofs where it builds its enormous nests. The Germans and Poles used indeed to erect special platforms, a cartwheel perhaps, to help the birds find a suitable base for the masses of nesting material they use (in which house-sparrows often nest—sometimes a dozen or more). Though never an 'inner-city' dweller, the white stork for long frequented smaller towns and was always looked upon affectionately because of the old legend about its bringing babies, while in addition it, too, paid its rent by acting as a scavenger, though frogs and snakes find their way into its maw also.

Like all the family, the white stork is remarkable because it is dumb. It possesses no vocal muscles. All it can do is clack its long red spear of a bill. Sometimes, especially in the breeding season, this clacking is so loud that it can be heard even when the birds are no longer in sight, for storks enjoy soaring far up in the thermals, high above the towns or villages they still visit. During the autumnal migration particularly they are sometimes to be seen over the region of Istanbul, in company with scores of high-flying vultures in what, if I dare put it thus, is pure enjoyment of their mastery of the air.

But the recorded numbers of the stork in Europe are like the tolling of a bell. In recent years in the Netherlands, for example, only six nests have been noted; in Alsace, fewer than two dozen; in Denmark, sixty-five, though happily in Germany, Austria and Poland there have been small increases.

The animal tenants of town houses are by no means confined to reptiles and lizards and birds. There is an abundance of mammals, too—chiefly the rats and mice which will be dealt with presently. They are of course scroungers, squatters, paying not a ha'porth of rent. Occasionally there are unexpected, almost freakish rodent visitors, examples of how nature is always ready to make use of man (or is it simply a question of man happen-

Usually a male swift returns a day or two before his mate in spring. Both accomplish a six-thousand-mile journey from South Africa.

A stork's nest, added to each year, has sometimes contained nearly a
hundredweight of material and measured eight feet in diameter
and as much in depth.

ing to be in the way, anything appertaining to him being as naturally
acceptable to the animals as tree or burrow or berry or insect?). Staying in
an hotel in the Lapland city of Rovaniemi, I have seen lemmings standing
up aggressively, to the full extent of their six inches, to an indignant
Finnish chambermaid attacking them with a broom. These strange,
tortoiseshell-patterned little rodents are best-known for the periodical
irruptions that occur, when literally millions of them make their way in
panic across the fells, harried by innumerable predators, snowy owl, fox,
wolverene, weasel, marten, buzzard, short-eared owl, all of whose numbers
increase, too, because of the easy feeding they enjoy at the expense of the
teeming hordes. In some years even a town such as Oslo has been invaded
by wandering lemmings, while twenty years ago houses in the Swedish
town of Ostersund were beset by the lemmings in search of food. At times
during the last century lemmings invading houses in Trondheim were so
persistent that people tried to catch them by means of wooden planks
thickly coated with tar.

One mammal that does pay an honest rent for its residence in many a
town house or building is the bat. Bats have intrigued us throughout the
ages. Many superstitions and legends surround them. They were feared
because of their sinister appearance and uncanny habitat such as church

towers and darksome lofts; even their disturbing habit of hanging upside down when at rest. Women were afraid they might become entangled in their hair. Bats shared with toads and newts the reputation of being the familiars of witches.

Besides, men didn't know what manner of creature the bat was. Only in the sixteenth century did the French naturalist Pierre Belon, by dissecting a specimen, establish that it was not a bird but a mammal. Only in the eighteenth century did the Italian Lazaro Spallanzani, somewhat brutally, prove that the bat did not rely on sight for its expert, pin-point navigating. He blinded a number of bats and found that they could perfectly well manoeuvre in flight now they were truly blind. But not until the present century was it established that the bat possesses a kind of ultrasonic equipment. It is able to send out short-wavelength squeaks or pulses, the reflected echoes from which provide information about the nature and position of surrounding objects. These squeaks are sent out at about thirty per second, and the faster the squeak-rate, the more information comes back to the flying bat.

Even in London, long-eared bats—Leisler's, serotine, noctule (whose dashing flight is reminiscent of the swift's) and pipistrelle, smallest of English bats, have been recorded, for they can still earn a living in some of the parks. In America the commonest town bat is the mouse-eared little brown bat which frequently sets up home in the attics of houses, sometimes joined by its larger relation the big brown bat. Many a householder, unbeknown to himself, has a number of bat-tenants in the nooks and crevices of his rafters, and few local churches are without them, literally in the belfry. Bats make their exits and entrances as subtly as falling leaves; but if there are too many of them, olfactory evidence becomes more obvious.

As for the invertebrate 'wildlife' occupants of town-houses and offices and factories and eating-houses and so on—and many of which form the prey of the other household tenants we have mentioned—their names are legion and would be impossible fully to enumerate here.

The tortoiseshell butterfly which hibernates by the dozen in the attics of houses, to emerge wanly in the spring sunshine and end its brief career—the earwig, subject of gruesome but ludicrous legends of entering human ears and burrowing into the brain—the clothes-moth, despair of many a housewife—the death-watch beetle, whose sinister noise is caused by its striking its head against the woodwork on which the grubs feed for years on end—the chirruping house-cricket, originally given its more familiar name by John Milton in *Il Penseroso*—

> Far from all resort of mirth,
> Save the cricket on the hearth!

41

—the wood-louse, ants, bluebottles, houseflies, the extraordinary fire-brat and its cousin the silver-fish, members of the bristletail family, that dart about among many a storecupboard feasting on spilt sugar or even going all intellectual and devouring weighty tomes in the library. While the common house-flea, *Pulex irritans*, warrants a place, though it is no longer 'common'; the bed-bug too, which, in Pliny's ancient times, was, macerated in wine, used as a medicine, even as an antidote to snake-bite. And surely the louse—the human louse, for there are many others—should be included. For, ironically, in these hygienic times, there has been a recrudescence of lice, especially head-lice, among children in certain English towns. The louse has for long been the subject of a certain type of humour but it is an historic creature because of its connection with typhus which, in many a war and disaster, has caused more casualties than have the cannons and the bombs.

During the Thirty Years' War in the seventeenth century, for example, Gustavus Adolphus and Wallenstein had to abandon a projected battle near Nuremberg because 18,000 of their troops had died of louse-borne typhus. Even in everyday life the louse played an important role: French royal children were exhorted by their tutor not to scratch for lice while in company, which echoes the advice George Washington received in his school-primer, *Rules in Civility*, that it was bad manners to kill vermin such as lice or fleas 'in the sight of others'.

Truly, you could compile an extensive natural history without ever stirring from your own dwelling! The arachnologist alone would be kept busy studying the spiders which range from the common house-spider to the long-legged, menacing-looking but harmless monsters that cause such domestic consternation when found in the bath or the kitchen-sink. Apart from these, one or two unusual spiders are sometimes recorded in cities, such as the *Segestria florentina*. Not by any means do all spiders use a web for catching their prey; the *Segestria*, for example, ensconces itself in a silken tub in a wall-crevice, from which it rushes out on its prey. And altogether the spiders that inhabit human dwellings are among the most useful tenants you could wish for; they certainly pay their rent through the flies they trap.

It should perhaps be said here that the spider, unlike most of the other household guests we have mentioned, is not an insect. It has only two body sections and has four pairs of legs, whereas a true insect in the adult state has a body divided into three distinct sections or regions. These are the head, with feelers or antennae and three pairs of jaws; the thorax or middle region, to which usually two or three pairs of legs are attached, and then the abdomen.

But all—insects and arachnids—are arthropods, that is to say, animals with jointed limbs.

One of the most remarkable of the innumerable and lowly town-

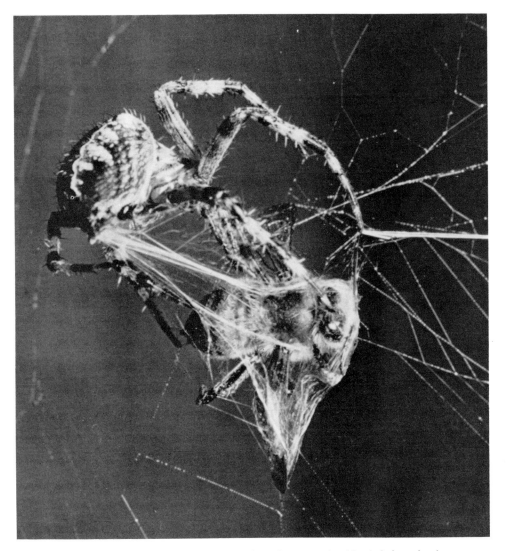

Spiders paralyse their victims by means of a poison contained in their jaw glands. Few spiders in the world are dangerous to humans; none in Britain.

dwellers, which perhaps deserves a postscript to itself, is the cockroach— whose range extends from New York to Novosibirsk and from Birmingham to Bombay, having always been an inveterate traveller. It is popularly dubbed a 'black beetle', a double error, for it is neither black nor a beetle. In fact, it is often a glossy brown and is more closely allied to the grass- hoppers. But instead of being renowned for its saltatory powers, it is famed

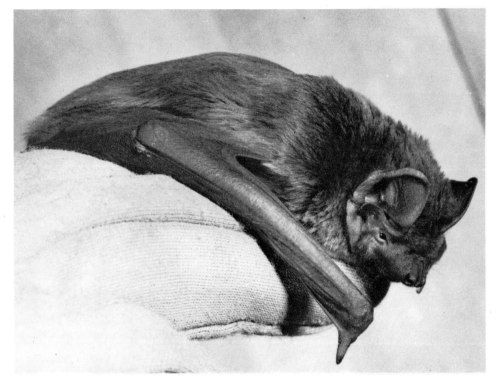

The noctule or great bat is the largest European species, having a wing-span of fifteen inches. It flies mainly at sunset and dawn, at very great heights.

as a runner. Although it has wings of a sort, it hardly ever flies, except in a rather drunken fashion, but to compensate for that it is probably the swiftest runner in the insect world. Added to which it has ultra-sensitive warning devices in its knee-caps, with the result that the irate householder usually gets only a fleeting glimpse of a shiny, almost varnished-looking body scuttling back into the wainscot or the floorboards.

The cockroach achieved literary fame some sixty years ago, when Don Marquis, columnist of the New York *Evening Sun*, created a cockroach philosopher-hero named archy, one of whose pronouncements was 'i will admit that some of the insects do not lead noble lives but is every man s hand to be against them yours for less justice and more charity' (archy s typing was not his strong point).

Well, in spite of archy s plea, cockroaches aren't in need of charity. While the more obvious household pests such as rats and mice draw down our imprecations, the cockroach goes its nefarious ways in kitchen and bathroom and restaurant and bakery and ship—and can also spread diseases such as typhoid. It is estimated that unchecked a pair of cockroaches and their progeny could produce half a million others yearly. But though there are perhaps 3500 known species, the vast majority prefer the great outdoors; only some half dozen having realized what a cinch life with *Homo sapiens* can be.

Of the really 'notorious' species, the small German cockroach is the commonest, a real internationalist. The American cockroach is nick-named the ship's cockroach, though like any sailor it is quite prepared to go on the spree in town. But probably the most familiar in town-buildings all over Europe and America is the Oriental cockroach, large, flat, an inch and a half long, of a very dark glossy sandy colour, and with long, curved antennae.

The cockroach is prepared to sample anything and everything, from cheese to wall-paper. It ruined the bread-fruit Captain Bligh was bringing home in the *Bounty*. What is more, the cockroach is equipped to pre-taste any item before actually eating it, in case some householder has had nasty ideas. But it is not the amount of food the myriad cockroaches of the world consume that matters. It is the quantities they ruin simply by tainting them with their ghastly odour which makes the food uneatable.

On one point Don Marquis's archy was correct. This was when he claimed that 'insects were insects when man was only a burbling whatsit. i do not know why man should be so proud', for it has been shown through fossil remains that cockroaches in almost exactly the same form existed more than three hundred million years ago.

This cockroach is not processing a kind of Gruyère cheese but munching away at a piece of bread.

45

CHAPTER FOUR

Garden-party

It is not only our houses nature moves into. An aerial photograph of any town reveals a patchwork of gardens and parks, leafy squares and churchyards and allotments, unnoticed from street-level. All of them are little oases amid the concrete desert, refuges for bird and insect and wild-flower.

Numerous though are 'the little, meagre, shrivelled, hopping, though loud and troublesome insects of the hour' (Edmund Burke's words in another context) that pursue their myriad way through urban dwellings, munching at the woodwork, tidying up microscopic particles, preying on each other in the jungle of wainscot and closet and rafter, it is of course in the open that insects—and other wildlife—more abundantly flourish.

They do so in spite of all the poisons employed by the gardener in pursuit of his notion of beauty, regardless of the fact that in the process he helps to destroy other more natural beauty—and in spite of the fetish for neatness which demands that lawns should be as shaven as the scalp of a skinhead and flowerbeds as artificially arranged as if they were some floral parade ground. Every gardener and park-keeper should be obliged to learn and take to heart Gerard Manley Hopkins's words—

> What would the world be, once bereft
> Of wet and wildness? Let them be left,
> O let them be left, wildness and wet;
> Long live the weeds and the wilderness yet.

If we let in the wilderness a little more, in however modest a way, nature would respond gratefully. The song-thrush would smash the snails for us on his stone anvil. The blackbird would spread the snowdrop bulbs for us by his foraging. Tortoiseshells and swallowtails would lay their eggs on the nettles. Slow-worm and frog and toad would keep down the slugs—though they would need to keep a careful look-out for the hedgehogs that still here and there inhabit city parks and commons. The bees would pollinate our flowers and in so doing improve the local ecology through an increase in seeds and berries and other food for different species of small-scale wildlife.

And at the same time those bees, even in built-up areas, produce honey for their owners—indeed, it is a nice irony that, partly because of the greater freedom from herbicides and crop-spraying, bees in towns often do better than their rural counterparts which are always at the mercy of the chemical-crazy farmer. In Inner London, for example, in such unlikely haunts as Oxford Street and Piccadilly, there are nearly two hundred bee-keepers, their hives installed on balcony and roof. As for Greater London, well over sixteen hundred bee-keepers own nearly five thousand hive-colonies, some of these hives producing an astonishing amount of honey, occasionally up to 150 lbs each, three times as much as many rural hives.

These London bees work mainly in the parks and gardens and tree-lined streets and squares, gathering their nectar from a variety of sources, chestnut and mulberry and privet and virginia creeper and especially that loveliest of trees, the lime, in addition to all the many garden flowers and the flowers in the thousands of window-boxes kept by nature-hungry citizens. Centuries ago someone wrote that 'a bee among the flowers is one of the cheerfullest objects that can be looked upon. Its life appears to be all enjoyment, so busy and pleased is it.' It is certainly pleasant for us to

According to Laurens van der Post, the bushmen of the Kalahari regard the praying mantis as the sun god, creator and guardian of life. French peasants were afraid to kill the insect because, in Thomas Hood's words, 'it lifts its paws most parson-like'.

envisage those millions of industrious, peerless insects (each colony contains about forty thousand bees) winging their tireless way to and fro above a great city, distilling from the flowers their incomparable food—which man through the ages has filched from them. Professor Arthur Thomson once calculated that worker bees from one hive would visit more than a quarter of a million flowers in a single day, each bee on each journey fetching a load of nectar equivalent to half its own weight.

Fortunate the suburban householder who can with John Milton hide from 'day's garish eye'

> While the bee with honied thigh
> That at her flowery work doth sing,

though this sentiment might not find approval among the inhabitants of Brazil's cities, where the notorious killer bees—result of trying to increase honey production by crossing a native breed with a Tanzanian one— truly live up to their name.

But, returning to insects in general—in spite of all the handicaps, pollution included, insects inhabiting urban areas still hold their own. Ladybird, centipede, wire-worm, cockchafer, bumble-bee, mason-wasp, stag-beetle, thrip, grasshopper, and all the rest, they form only an infinitesimal proportion of the 650,000 insects species in the world (with another 3000 being discovered every year); nevertheless it would be impossible to catalogue them here: we might mention in this context the work of Dr Frank Lutz, one-time Curator of Entomology in the American Museum of Natural History. In his tiny garden in Ramsey, New Jersey, he identified more than 1400 species of insect, ranging from cicadas to ant-lions and from saw-flies to spring-tails—which needed a whole book, *A Lot of Insects*, to accommodate.

There are two or three garden animals I find especially interesting for very different reasons. The word animal is appropriate here partly because we tend to use it only in connection with mammals, whereas of course all creatures with the power of independent movement are animals, from the tiniest freshwater shrimp to the mighty blue whale, and partly because the first of these garden creatures I have in mind isn't an insect. This is the spider, its difference from the insects mentioned earlier.

The spider's web is one of the most beautiful constructions in nature; also one of the most efficient traps. Compare this intricate device, drawn from the body of this 'lowly' creature, with the ugly snares men still use: the clumsy fall-trap that crushes the victim or the staked pit-trap that mutilates it. Subtly the spider waits for the message conveyed by the trembling of its silken thread—

> The spider's web, how exquisitely fine!
> Feels at each thread, and lives along the line.

Of course, as we also mentioned before, not by any means do all spiders construct webs. But some, often to be found in urban gardens, employ a simple but highly ingenious piece of apparatus. When the tiny zebra spider, for example, goes hunting among walls and banks, it trails behind it a kind of dragline with which it takes a purchase here and there. Should it stumble or miss its jump, the dragline saves it from falling. No mountaineer's rope could be better; moreover, it was possibly from this dragline that long ages ago the spider's web itself evolved.

In order to survive, the stick insect (of which there are many kinds) simply imitates the vegetation it lives on. It is indeed one of the most remarkable examples of protective camouflage. With its very long, thin, cylindrical body—some species are up to twelve inches in length—it lies totally motionless throughout the day along the branch of shrub or climbing rose, with its gawky, angular legs exactly resembling the twigs amongst which it mingles. And the human observer peers and peers again, trying to discern these weird illustrations of nature's cunning which have survived only by means of this imitative faculty.

Mostly the Phasmidae or stick insects exist in tropical countries, in India notably, but they do frequent gardens in southern Europe and in parts of Canada and the United States—where they are called walking-sticks. But intriguing though the stick insect is (some people have tried keeping it as a pet, not a very satisfactory one as it only bestirs itself at night to do its leaf-eating), a far more dramatic garden insect in southern climes is the praying mantis, pale green in colour and with long gauzy wings. Those stick insects would be—and often are!—easy meat for it, as indeed are many other species—so much so that an enterprising American on Long Island set up a business supplying gardeners with mantis eggs which, as they hatched out, would be an unrivalled aid against insect pests.

The mantis is one of the most ferocious of insects—the female being by far the more formidable and it is among the largest of European insects, reaching a good three inches in length at times. The word mantis comes from the Greek for prophet, while the descriptive adjective derives from its habit of standing half erect with forelegs lifted like hands raised in supplication—the scientific name for the species being *Mantis religiosa*. What is more, the mantis really has what might be called a face and its strangely disturbing stare is enhanced by the fact that it has a flexible neck, enabling it to move its head in any direction. It is the only insect that can bend its gaze wherever it chooses.

But in the words of J. H. Fabre, incomparable entomologist of the garden, those pious airs are a fraud; those arms raised in prayer are actually the most murderous weapons, which slay whatever passes, including eventually the female mantis's mate, for 'she is worse than the wolf; even wolves never devour each other'. 'Fierce as a tiger, cruel as an ogress'

49

though this strange creature may be, I have to admit to having watched in fascination many times in a garden in Montpellier as one of these mantises went about its work.

Marvellous and beautiful are nature's creations, but nothing is more remarkable than the machinery of an insect's body. 'The haunch of the mantis is very long and powerful,' wrote Fabre, 'while the thigh is even longer, and carries on its lower surface two rows of sharp spikes or teeth. Behind these teeth are three spurs. In other words, the thigh is a saw with two blades, between which the leg lies when folded back. This leg itself is also a double-edged saw, provided with a greater number of teeth than the thigh. It ends in a strong hook with a point as sharp as a needle, and a double blade like a curved pruning-knife. When at rest, the trap is folded back against the chest and looks perfectly harmless. The mantis is at prayer! But if a victim passes, its devotions are speedily abandoned. The three long divisions of the trap are swiftly unfolded, and the prey is caught with the sharp hook, and drawn back between the two saws.'

How long was it before man invented comparable machinery!— though as far as weaponry is concerned he has now far surpassed the insects in his fearful devices.

It has to be admitted that there is a certain chilling air about the praying mantis as it seems to stare at you like some science-fiction creature. There are, superficially, at least, more attractive insect-denizens of the town—the Lepidoptera, the butterflies and moths—though some of these have rather unsavoury tastes, such as animal dung or putrid meat.

Altogether of course the Lepidoptera are less numerous than other insects: Dr Lutz for instance could list only thirty-five butterflies in his New Jersey garden, though these did include such beauties as the black swallowtail and the regal fritillary. Even in central London it is possible to sight species as varied as the peacock and the red admiral and the painted lady, possibly feasting at some honey-scented buddleia, while vapourer moths often flicker round the street-lamps and the exceedingly handsome elephant hawk-moth has often been found on the rosebay willow-herb that colonized bomb-sites.

Some of the butterflies visiting urban areas are spectacularly beautiful and in this connection I always remember a letter from a friend who was visiting America. It was full of the wonders of the West, from the New York skyline to the Grand Canyon. But one thing above all that had delighted her was the monarch butterflies in the neighbourhood of San Francisco. These are some of the loveliest wild visitors any townsman could wish to see—vividly striking, chestnut-brown creatures with prominent veins on their four-inch wings.

But their most remarkable characteristic is their annual migrations. Regularly in spring and autumn they travel to and fro across the North

The American monarch or milkweed butterfly has performed some remarkable feats of migration. In 1840 it was reported in New Zealand, thirty years later in Australia, and in 1880 it was seen in the Canary Islands.

American continent from California and Louisiana and Florida all the way to regions such as Hudson Bay in Canada. At times these migrations involve millions of butterflies, and if there is wonder in bird-migration, one can only be astonished at the transcontinental journeys achieved by such frail butterflies. 'Impotent and grovelling insect' indeed!

My friend had seen these monarchs (or milkweeds as they are also called, from the plant on which their eggs are laid and their caterpillars feed) after they returned from their subarctic trip. Along with many citizens of San Francisco, she had gone out to Stinson Beach where untold thousands of monarchs settle on 'butterfly trees', rank upon rank, fold upon fold of breath-taking beauty created by all those assembled satiny wings, a

51

fairy-land array of dreamlike character, for which awed silence was the only possible tribute.

And in those trees the monarchs pass the winter in semi-hibernation, until a little greater warmth from the sun sends them fluttering around for a while, filling the air with glinting shards of beauty, drifting, flitting in faintly bewildered fashion, as if the butterflies were flying in their sleep, until they settle back on the trees again. So valued were these charming visitors that you could be fined five hundred dollars for wilfully disturbing them, my friend added approvingly.

Very rarely has the monarch occurred in Britain, and then possibly through being carried on the wind or as a 'stowaway' on board ship. Another lovely butterfly migrant which very occasionally arrived in Britain may also do so by the same means: the Camberwell beauty. With its almost sombre, dark purple wings edged with creamy yellow, the mourning-cloak butterfly, as it is known in its native Scandinavia and America, has never been known to breed in Britain, but two hundred years ago it appeared in such 'prodigious' numbers, as a contemporary entomologist put it, that it was called the grand surprise. It was also nicely called white petticoat, while another name for it was willow beauty because of its favourite food-tree.

It has occasionally turned up in London—in Hampstead and Balham and the nearby borough from which it derives its usual English name, while a few years ago one was observed sunning itself on a motorcar in the city. In Scandinavia it often hibernates among stacks of logs and sawn planks, so it is quite feasible that it has arrived in London on board a timber-ship.

Nature in city gardens and parks varies as much as such 'refuges' themselves do: from the half-tame peacocks, whose raucous caterwauling jars with their flaunting splendour in Cochin or Madura or Mangalore, to the blackbird uttering his mellifluous phrases from a television aerial in Tooting or Beckenham.

In the tropics nature is inevitably lusher, more varied, more strident than in temperate climes. The colour seems to join in with the sun in aiming stunning blows at you. But even in some Indian cities, where the turbulent flood of humanity flowed all round, you could not fail to wonder at it, however much you saw of it. It was as if nature, taking pity on man, was endeavouring to disguise all the ugliness he perpetrated by draping the veil of her beauty over everything.

Arriving at a railroad station you were often greeted by the sight of the well-named railway creeper or porter's joy, that cousin of the morning glory, whose dreamlike, mauve, salver-shaped flowers seemed to be flung everywhere, like prodigal, welcoming garlands. On all sides, garden fences and walls were covered with masses of bougainvillea, whose colours of magenta or purple or crimson or yellow came not, as you might think, from the flowers but from the bracts that surrounded the flowers themselves. Jacaranda, *gul mohr*, golden shower, madre, tulip-tree, nim tree, coral-creeper and so many others—all in one way or another added to the wonderful, dazzling kaleidoscope everywhere you turned. It was a visual experience that was transmuted into an inward vision never to fade. And I have one memory of a Hindu temple-garden—a pool of tranquillity in the midst of a brutal, ever-swirling human maelstrom outside—where the fragrant petals of the frangipani tree, emblem of immortality because it blooms almost throughout the year, were floating down to the steely surface of the fish-pond, to lie like waxen shallops until nosed aside in a mad rush as scores of huge mahseer came swirling towards the bank, hoping to be fed. Even in 'mid-winter', when there were otherwise few flowers, many gardens glowed with the brilliant bracts of the poinsettia—named after the Honourable Poinsett of South Carolina, a nineteenth-century American ambassador, who brought the shrub from Mexico. And it has a nickname, Christmas plant, because of the season when it flowers.

The contrast with the plant-life that finds a foothold in western streets and squares and building-lots could not be greater. And yet, much as one has admired and marvelled at all the dramatic botanical splendour of the Orient, this has sometimes seemed almost overpowering, almost contrived, a brash *coup de théâtre*. Western cities have their magnificent trees—such as the stately redwoods or the Ponderosa pines of San Francisco—or those glorious horse-chestnuts which in season light up the Champs Elysées with their candles—or the Lombardy poplars and the handsome London plane of the English capital—or the big-tooth aspens and Chinese elms and the ailanthus, alias tree of heaven of New York, which the short-story writer O. Henry called a 'backyard tree', though a young ailanthus can put on eight feet of growth in a year.

But the wildflowers that struggle to take root in the city are often so humble as to pass unnoticed except by the observant eye. Yet a list of them sounds like a catalogue from some country lane—horehound, red dead nettle, wild barley, meadow foxtail, cat's ear, hawkbit, goosegrass, woody nightshade, corn bindweed, knapweed, sow-thistle, fever-few—all these and innumerable others have crept in to London, for example, their seeds windborne or carried by birds or even on the boots of people who have been out in the country: reminding one of Charles Darwin detaching the soil from the leg of a dead partridge he had been sent and subsequently identifying eighty-two plants which grew from the seeds it contained.

Similarly with some animals the embankments of railway commuter lines are among the best refuges for wild plants—bracken, with its tall, cool stands, the lovely 'male' fern, sometimes known as deadman's hands from the likeness of its unfurling frond-buds to a clenched fist, wall rocket, cow parsley, and that strange and imposing plant, the giant hogweed, which

Nature literally red in tooth and claw—as exemplified by this incident recorded
by a French magazine of a girl with a basket of fish attacked
by starving alley- cats.

Beautiful and cunning, the fox is also supremely adaptable—shown by the way it
coped when myxomatosis drastically reduced the rabbit population. It should be
quite at home among the dustbins, for it has little sanitary sense, leaving litter
outside its earth and fouling the interior in a way no badger would tolerate.

The robin's bizarre choice of nesting sites is traditional. One pair even nested in
a church pulpit undisturbed by parson, choir or organ.

can reach nine or ten feet, and is beloved of a variety of insects but whose juice can bring up fierce blisters on human skin—often when children have tried to make a rustic pipe out of its thick, hollow stem.

Some plants that have unexpectedly sprung up in city areas are illustrative of nature's never-failing opportunism—vines and cherries and plums and apples that have secretly established themselves long after pip or stone has been left from some office-worker's snack. Seed from bird-tables is never wasted, even if the birds themselves have scattered it and failed to retrieve it. Many handsome grasses have sprung up as a result. Even the notorious hemp that sometimes appears on waste land has happened thus.

Many urban flora are so small and insignificant they have to be looked for, hidden as they are in ruined wall and crevice and flagged pathway, like certain exquisite, tiny sea shells that remain concealed among the predominant shingle; but all are gems of nature, and within the boundaries of town or city there is as much scope for the botanist as for the entomologist.

But if the Indian gardens we mentioned are drenched in unrivalled colour, where English cities score is in the question of bird-song. Constantly through those eastern trees passed and passed again all the many birds whose flashing wings added to the palimpsest of colour: golden orioles, dramatically black and yellow, the silky gold-fronted chloropsis, yellow-throated sparrows, the tailor-bird crying *pretty pretty*, the myna that yells *radio radio radio* as if it were an avian transistor, the bulbuls that often raided the kitchens for scraps—and were more welcome than the Hanuman monkeys.

Yet beautiful though are all these birds and many others, and joyous their shrill notes, few of them commanded any real song: their extravagant colours seem to do proxy for this. Even the strikingly handsome, silvery white paradise flycatcher, with its black-crested head and two long tail-streamers, can only muster a harsh, grating call, while the charming little 'Shoubeegi' or common iora manages little more than a chorus of musical whistles—reminiscent of that accomplished American whistler, the red cardinal. There are exceptions to this concept of beauty being a substitute for song. For example, that most attractive American bird, to be seen occasionally on city outskirts, the scarlet tanager, is also one of the most persistent singers, while the rose-breasted crossbeak, frequent visitor to New York parks, is both beautiful and melodious. And the European robin, John Donne's 'household bird, with the red Stomacher', is as well-known for its glorious patch of flame as for its spring and autumn threnody.

Generally speaking, however, in a country such as Britain, the best singers are modestly, sometimes soberly feathered. The stumpy little wren, whose explosive, challenging, incredibly powerful song can be heard in Inner London—the song-thrush whose wild, ecstatic, extemporizing gladdens many a suburban garden—the blackbird, with its marvellous, placid, mellow, contented fluting—the woodlark, whose exuberant song can occasionally be heard and its joyous flight seen on some town commons (and once upon a time in Richmond Park)—even the willow warbler, whose song the 'Hudson River' naturalist John Burroughs once described as having 'a dying fall: no other bird song is so touching in this respect. It mounts up round and full, then runs down the scale and expires upon the air in a gentle murmur'—it is for their songs these and similar birds are remarked, not for their colours.

But the classic example of song taking the place of vivid colour is the nightingale. This migrant cousin of the robin, who comes to us every year from north-west Africa, and can still be heard, alas, less and less, in a few English suburbs and commons, is in fact a rather drab, skulking little bird whose long-drawn, plaintive, almost sobbing notes still have the power to hold us breathless and strangely moved.

A discovery I made long ago was what marvellous wildlife refuges some graveyards can be. I used to stay with an aunt in a large town on the south coast of England. One boy who made friends with me lived at a fair distance, but in the course of time it was thought fit for me to find my own way home even at night—the evening, that's to say. A neighbouring churchyard offered a short cut, but for long the detour of half a mile was infinitely preferable to venturing through that awful place. In the light of a street-lamp, the shadows of a solitary yew tree loomed like a dark shroud ready to stifle any intruder, while the tombstones themselves seemed like trap-doors in a nightmare leading down to who knows what horrors.

One night, however, I was very late—censoriously the church clock was just tolling ten!—ten o'clock—my aunt would have a fit!—and so, on the spur of the moment, I pushed open the scruppeting iron gate and climbed the mossy steps leading from the street, for the churchyard was much higher than the pavement—perhaps because of plague burials which had caused the surface to be raised to accommodate all the additional tenants. Most of the way from my friend's house I had been running; but now, no doubt discreetly afraid of raising the dead, I walked reverently, tiptoed almost, along the path between the ghostly memorials, my scalp tingling in rebuttal of Swinburne's claim that 'dead men rise up never!' Even the occasional motorcar seemed to be hurrying past to get clear of the danger zone.

Suddenly I froze—and now I could verily have confirmed Clarence's words in *Richard III*: 'so full of dismal terror was the time!' At the base of a hideous, gigantic mausoleum, raised to the memory of some probably unworthy burgess, an invisible presence was moving. It was making quite a noise, shuffling among leaves and debris—it even snuffled (could ghosts catch cold?)—and I could hear a furtive clicking. To my fevered imagination it was as if a stone lid was being slowly forced open to allow some grisly revenant to emerge. If ever I knew the truth of being 'rooted to the spot', it was then. In my palsied hand the torch flickered, probed the sky like a miniature searchlight—anywhere but in the right direction. But at length I forced it to focus on the undoubted horror that lay before me.

Only gradually did relief replace astonishment. That apparently sinister bustling sound was made by a hedgehog going about his lawful occasions, foraging for all the rich harvest of slugs and snails and beetles and wood-lice and earthworms which, like him, were among the teeming— I didn't yet realize how appropriate was the word—wildlife of that church-yard and many another elsewhere.

I went back to the place in daytime, in the hope of encountering the hedgehog again. I was disappointed, but sometimes on warm days slow-worms, those grossly misnamed and beautiful legless lizards, used to bask in their bronzy loveliness in the sun. All round in the unkempt grass—for it was an ill-tended graveyard—grasshoppers fiddled away. A sycamore, whose branches tapped against one of the stained glass windows, was loud with the grateful hymn of thousands of bees and bumble-bees and other insects. A demure, ash-brown, rather quakerish bird—after due reference to T. A. Coward I identified it as a spotted flycatcher—sallied out from its vantage point on a marble cross, the tiny click of its bill audible as it snapped up passing flies. Out of the corner of another tomb a trickle of ants came and went, as sedulous in their own minute world as the townsfolk walking along the pavement outside. A tortoiseshell butterfly actually savoured some newly offered flowers from a recent burial. A blackbird went shrieking hysterically away from its nest in a laurel bush. Indeed, flashing wings seemed constantly to be passing on all sides, and in the yew tree a thrush began to sing.

> With glee, with glee, with glee,
>   Cheer up, cheer up, cheer up, here
> Nothing to harm us, then sing merrily,
>   Sing to the loved ones whose nest is near—
> *Qui, qui, qui, kweeu quip,*
>   *Tiurru, tiurru, chipiwi,*
>   *Too-tee, too-tee, chiuchoo,*
>   *Chirri, chirri, chooee,*
>   *Quiu, qui, qui.*

Needless to say, it didn't occur to me at the time, or on other occasions there, but really it was all such a splendid mockery of the tawdry stone and marble memorials, the odious cherubs and the angels with rolling eyes. How much more cheerful to have those birds singing and darting above your mortal remains and your gravestone covered with a rich golden

It is said that the mistle-thrush got its name from its habit of feeding on mistletoe berries. But it has also been dubbed the butcher-boy of the woods because of its pugnacity in defending its nest.

patina of lichen. That thrush had more to say than the trite epitaphs carved on the doom-heavy headstones. (And incidentally surely nobody has ever improved on the eighteenth-century William Macgillivray's rendering of the thrush's song.)

So my encounter with the hedgehog not only cured me of my terrors, it made me appreciate ever afterwards what miniature wildlife sanctuaries churchyards can be, even in the midst of crowded towns. And of course the churches themselves invariably have their wild tenants—bats that flit out quiet as falling leaves from the belfries—the jackdaws that stridently say their matins round the gargoyles of Notre Dame—the swifts that race and wheel in shrill delight round many a church steeple—while on the sun-warmed walls of Mediterranean churches you can often count a couple of dozen lizards worshipping in their own particular way.

It goes almost without saying that owls have often taken advantage of

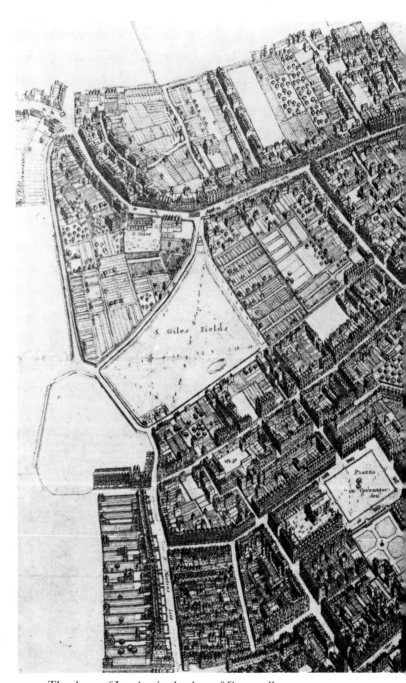

The shape of London in the days of Cromwell.
Parks and open spaces, private gardens and vegetable plots
all provided a habitat for nature in the city.

the furry residents that creep about churchyards and the sparrows that roost in ivy-clad walls. Tawny owls have been more frequent town-dwellers, their lovely quavering hoot sometimes only a vague hint above the traffic, while in American graveyards the sweet whistling cry of the screech-owl can sometimes be heard. Its numbers nationwide greatly depleted, only occasionally now does the barn owl in England take up residence in a suburban church, sometimes, until its identity has been veri-fied, causing the sort of consternation Gilbert White described—'for the white owl does indeed snore and hiss in a tremendous manner and I have known a whole population up in arms on such occasions, imagining the churchyard to be full of goblins and spectres, the people believing the screech-owl attends the windows of dying persons'.

One unusual avian visitation to a churchyard was reported by Philip Gosse in the Dutch town of Delft. 'Suddenly a soft and winnowing sound in the air attracted his attention and, looking up, with involuntary thoughts of angels and spiritual visitants, he saw two white-winged beings hovering in the air, who presently descended and alighted close by. They were storks!—attracted, doubtless, to the moist and rank herbage by the expectation of a plentiful repast on insects and slugs which the dews had drawn abroad in the twilight.'

Someone should pick out a suitable town churchyard and study the ecology of it. Certainly it would be worthwhile and a gratifying list of wildlife would be revealed. From the London plane, which cleanses itself from pollution by shedding its bark regularly, to the beautiful maidenhair or ginkgo tree that grows in some American graveyards, from the Himalay-an balsam, found in their English counterparts to that lovely little pink, starry water-blink, an escape from America, from the humblest cockchafer and dor-beetle and cricket, through to bank-vole and shrew and mole— black-clad sexton if ever there was—toads, frogs, hedgehogs, and birds as varied as redstart and pied wagtail—while traditionally ladies in their Sunday best often had to run the gauntlet of rooks nesting in the elm trees that lined the path from the lychgate.

Graveyards in general, from the enormous suburban cemetery, big as a farm, to the garden-size resting-place, can be valuable oases of wildlife; indeed, modest areas of conservation in the surrounding desert of tarmac and concrete as important as a real oasis in the middle of a Saharan waste land. Valuable though parks are, they are, unavoidably, the scene of much human activity, children playing, dogs being exercised, whereas cemetery and graveyard are of necessity far more tranquil, less frequented, their alleyways flanked by tree and bush. Rabbits and squirrels breed in many urban cemeteries; mallard have raised their broods of ducklings in Bromp-ton cemetery; in Stuttgart, hares frolic over the tombstones, perhaps on a jaunt from the nearby Black Forest; in American towns, skunks and opossums are established residents of graveyards, discreetly emerging after dusk when any mourners have departed, while it has been known for clusters of chipmunks to hibernate together in the corner of some four-square tomb whose human occupants sleep even more soundly.

At times the potentialities of graveyards in this respect have been officially recognized. The American Nature Conservancy has turned a two-acre churchyard in California into a wildflower reserve, while in the east end of London the derelict twenty-seven-acre Tower Hamlet cemetery is now rich in bird life that enjoys the dense cover growing amid the rows of forgotten tombs. And the British Lichen Society has appealed 'to parishioners everywhere not to be too thorough when tidying up churchyards, particularly when scrubbing tombstones, which can support rare, years-old lichen growths'. The Society also called for restraint 'in pulling up "weeds" in neglected cemeteries, which are among the country's best nature reserves'.

As Tennyson puts it,

> . . . the mole has made his run,
> The hedgehog underneath the plantain bores,
> The rabbit fondles his own harmless face,
> The slow-worm creeps, and the thin weasel there
> Follows the mouse, as in an open field.

Though mainly aquatic, the water-shrew occasionally wanders far overland. As with other shrews, it seems likely that its bite contains certain toxic qualities.

CHAPTER FIVE

Dark Invader

One of the most historic examples of wildlife in the city is the rat, even though, as we shall see, this formidable animal is a comparative newcomer in the western world. But it has more than made up for lost time, thanks in large part to man's wasteful and unhygienic habits.

Like man himself, the rat, particularly the brown rat, is a worldwide colonizer. Not even the Antarctic is free from this most adaptable creature which has established itself on South Georgia, while with all the international geophysical activity it would not be surprising if one day it made it to the South Pole in somebody's snow-mobile. As for the Arctic, though it has so far left the Eskimos alone, it has long since set up home in habitats as bleak as Spitzbergen. In town areas I have seen it at work in places as disparate as the Promenade des Anglais in Nice and Hindu temples in Madras, protected there by the priests.

Yet in Europe the brown rat has been established for scarcely 250 years. According to the German naturalist Peter Simon Pallas (1741–1811), an enormous irruption of the species in the 1720s was caused by a series of earthquakes in its haunts east of the Caspian Sea. Hordes of rats swarmed across Russia and many of them took ship, literally, to Britain, there being an increasing commerce between the two countries, when Peter the Great 'opened his window on the west' in the shape of the city of Petersburg (the modern Leningrad) which he built on the Neva swampland.

Because of this shipborne invasion, the brown rat was mistakenly dubbed the Norwegian rat, while Stuart loyalists named it the Hanoverian rat, alleging that it had arrived in England in the self-same ship that brought the Elector of Hanover to the throne as George I on the basis of his tenuous relationship with the English monarchy. In fact, it was 1714 'when George in pudding time came o'er, And moderate men looked big, Sir', as the Vicar of Bray put it, whereas the brown rat followed some thirteen or fourteen years later.

Already established in Britain was the smaller black rat. This was said to have arrived in the thirteenth century in the ships of crusaders returning from Palestine. They brought back many useful things, or the knowledge of them, such as the lateen sail and windmills. The rat, however, was not such a desirable import. But in fact the species was also established on mainland Europe at the same time, suggesting that it had come overland.

Whatever the case, it had joyfully accepted the comparative bounty of

After the arrival of the aggressive brown rat, the black rat (shown here) became
so rare in the mid-nineteenth century that one ratcatcher was able to sell each
specimen he caught for three guineas to interested naturalists.

western man. There may have been a large patch of embroidery stitched
on to the well-known legend of the Rattenfanger von Hameln, the Pied
Piper of Hamelin, who, in revenge for being cheated of his rat-catching fee,
lured away the children of the town, but there is no reason to question the
basis of it—that is to say, the terrifying numbers of rats that soon swarmed
in the stews and alleys and houses of many towns where, in Robert Brown-
ing's words,

> Rats!
> They fought the dogs, and killed the cats,
>   And bit the babies in their cradles,
> And ate the cheeses out of the vats,
>   And licked the soup from the cooks' own ladles,
> Split open the kegs of salted sprats,
> Made nests inside men's Sunday hats,
> And even spoiled the women's chats,
>   By drowning their speaking
>   With shrieking and squeaking
> In fifty different sharps and flats.

Archibald Thorburn (1860–1935) was best known as an illustrator of birds. But his artistic merit coupled with scientific accuracy made him an accomplished painter of mammals, too.

—while in fourteenth-century England, Chaucer wrote in the *Pardoner's Tale*,

> And on he ran, he had no thought to tarry,
> Came to the town, found an apothecary,
> And said, 'Sell me some poison if you will,
> I have a lot of rats I want to kill'.

The black rat does not cause as much damage as its cousin for the simple reason that it is less numerous—and nowadays in English towns at least it is becoming a rare species, though in this case not even the most ardent conservationist has called for its protection. In another respect, the most serious charge against it was as a carrier of *Xenopsylla cheopis*, the flea which transmitted the fearful Black Death, though there were many other vectors, including the brown rat. For many centuries, sanitary conditions

66

were a constant menace to health: the putrefied blood of slaughtered
beasts was allowed to run in the streets, even barber-surgeons performing
the fashionable phlebotomy on their patients chucked the blood out into
the gutters, 'pudding-wives and tripe-wives' used to throw out paunches,
guts and entrails into the streets, human excrement piled up in the narrow
lanes and alleys. Droves of half-wild pigs roamed the town, verily in their
element.

Nevertheless, it is no coincidence that the plague which devastated
much of Western Europe broke out after the black rat had become established, bringing it from Asia—and more black rats were constantly arriving
by shipboard (in the course of time, rats took ship across the Atlantic and
arrived in America). The worst outbreak of Black Death in the mid-
fourteenth century is estimated to have killed a third of Europe's population. In Paris alone, deaths reached fifty thousand. Yet even 250 years later
in Elizabethan England, when the Black Death recurred with considerable
virulence, the rat was still not particularly suspected as a culprit. Everything else was looked upon with disfavour, including cats, pigs, rabbits,
pigeons, while special wardens were appointed in plague-time to 'murder'
and dispose of any dogs found loose in the streets. Daniel Defoe, writing
about the plague outbreak of 1665, reported that 40,000 dogs had been
slaughtered in London. Yet in the east, for long subject to the plague, the
rat had always been associated with the disease. In India it was reckoned
that a sure sign of the plague's being at hand was if a rat fell from the rafters,
jumped about on the floor in drunken fashion and died.

But the black rat went virtually free and continued to flourish in towns
such as London. Its numbers were only checked when the 'Hanoverian'
rat took over—replacing its smaller cousin in ever greater numbers and
committing far greater depredations. In England the black rat still hangs
on, but—apart from some pockets said to exist in the neighbourhood of
Oxford Circus—mainly in the Port of London, while it has always been a
more sea-going animal than the brown rat. In one year, for example,
2600 black rats were killed on ships in the port, as against only two browns.
But in London in general in one last-war drive, 650,000 rats were killed in a
single year, the vast majority of them brown rats. Such a figure, however,
pales into insignificance compared with the two million rats claimed to
have been killed in 1980 in one Egyptian governorate alone.

But in spite of such periodical campaigns, rats as urban animals still
flourish—sometimes in odd circumstances. The menagerie-entrepreneur,
Carl Hagenbeck, once had to destroy several of his Hamburg Zoo
elephants because rats had gnawed their feet so persistently, while some
years ago when keepers at the Regent's Park Zoo in London were puzzled
by the inexplicable restlessness of the elephants, they found that this was
also caused by rats nibbling their toes.

Many of the epithets applied to the rat are inaccurate. It certainly must be truly cunning, otherwise it would not have continued to infest the urban areas of the world in spite of all the measures taken against it. Intelligence rather than cunning might be more appropriate, as appreciated by the American farmer whom Sir James Frazer quoted as having written 'a civil letter to the rats, telling them that because his crops were short, he could not afford to keep them through the winter, that he had been very kind to them, and that for their own good he thought they had better leave him and go to some of his neighbours who had more grain. This document he pinned to a post in his barn for the rats to read.'

Leaving aside the rat's IQ, 'dirty' it certainly is not, scrupulously grooming itself, in spite or because of its liking for sewers. 'Old' rat is a misnomer, too, for it is doubtful whether the average age reaches more than eighteen months. Prudent and sensible it may be, as instanced in *The Tempest*—

> A rotten carcass of a boat, not rigged,
> Nor tackle, sail, nor mast; the very rats
> Instinctively have quit it—

but not cowardly, for it has often been known to stand up in desperation to ferret or stoat. What is more, the rat will often be the first to start hostilities. And there are many instances of rats attacking human beings—for example, a few years ago, in the town of Leamington in Ontario, rats bit to death a man who had fallen unconscious, while in the current plague of rats troubling Egypt there are many similar cases.

The two species are different in their preferred habitat. The black rat is sometimes also known as the climbing rat, being more arboreal and will even make its way along overhead power lines. It is more likely to be found in cavity walls and the roofs and lofts of warehouses and other buildings. The brown rat, on the other hand, although it can climb, is more at home in cellars and basements, sewers and rubbish dumps and the banks of canals (the misnamed water-rat is not a rat at all, and properly should be called the water-vole). So secretive and discreet is the brown rat in particular that many people are unaware of its existence in their own homes. Though if it gets into their garrets it may be more noticeable, for it is sometimes a noisy animal as it runs about overhead.

In every way the brown rat is by far the more formidable of the two. In many areas it has completely replaced the black rat, not merely by dint of numbers but by actually killing its cousin—one notable example being over a wide stretch of south-west Georgia in the United States. As Hans Zinsser put it, 'the gradual, relentless, progressive extermination of the black rat by the brown rat has no parallel in nature so close as that of the similar extermination of one race of man by another'.

The brown rat can be as much as two and a half times the weight of the black, reaching five hundred grams on occasions. In fact, size is one of the surest ways of distinguishing between the two species. For there is an occasional melanistic or black form of brown rat, while the Alexandrine rat, closely related to the black, is brown in colour. In addition, the black rat is more slender than the brown, has a finer coat and thinner, larger ears.

As for the rat's reproductive powers, the female starts breeding at three or four months, gestation is only three weeks, she can have as many as five or six litters a year, with up to ten young in each, and has often been found to be pregnant while still nursing the previous litter. Apart from being more prolific, the brown rat is bolder and more aggressive than its cousin. Richard Fitter recounts one instance concerning some rat-infested houses in London which were demolished partly as a means of solving the problem. The rats, disturbed over a long period and therefore in great hunger, not only invaded a neighbouring restaurant but actually competed with the horrified diners to the extent of jumping on to the tables and snatching food from the plates.

A literal example of the species being commensal with man.

As for the damage perpetrated by the brown rat in the cities and towns and urban areas of the world, it can only be said that this is incalculable and immense. What is certain is that millions more people could be fed if proper measures were taken to protect food-supplies such as rice and wheat against pests, chief of which is the brown rat.

Man has been both repelled and fascinated by the rat, that shadowy town-dweller which goes its furtive way 'between the dark and the daylight, when night is beginning to lower'—as Longfellow put it, though in a somewhat different context. This feeling has been prompted partly by the undoubted affinities between man and rat. Both have extended their habitat across the globe, almost keeping pace with one another. Both are the only creatures deliberately to make war against their own kind. Both are omnivorous. Both are capable of cannibalism in times of stress. Both are useless to other forms of life but themselves. Both breed at all seasons. Both have a remarkable degree of intelligence—J. B. S. Haldane thought that in the event of man disappearing from the face of the earth the rat would be his most likely successor. Both find their ever-increasing numbers a dangerous problem—and the rat, as with man, is forced to go on extending its range in order to survive. If man gets to the stars, the rat won't be far behind.

For the rat will probably never be exterminated. Years ago, in common with other experts, Dr Lantz of the United States Department of Agriculture estimated that in most cities there were as many rats as people and this is still near the mark. Already in Britain 'super rats' are a growing problem: ninety per cent have developed a resistance to some of the strongest poisons

Outbreaks of bubonic plague were largely caused by the black rat, the main carrier, encouraged by atrocious sanitary conditions. The well-to-do fled to the countryside; the less well-off perforce stayed put and died in their thousands. In the last great outbreak in 1665 Samuel Pepys recorded at least ten thousand deaths in a single week in the city of London. 'Partly from the poor that cannot be taken notice of through the greatness of their number, and partly from the Quakers and others that will not have any bell rung for them.' No animal has more gruesomely made its mark in history than the black rat.

such as Warfarin; twenty per cent are even immune to the much more potent anti-coagulant Difenacoum.

Perhaps the only effective way of reducing the rat population would be to adopt the suggestion of the poet Robert Southey that the rat should be regarded as a table delicacy. And, after all, in the Siege of Paris in 1871 rats fetched a high price among the starving people.

In the Italian city of Pisa, birth-control methods through chemicals causing sterilization have been tried out. But these take six months to act, while the matter was complicated by the installation of a new rubbish incinerator which deprived the rats of their staple diet. They promptly started to swarm into the city centre and the situation has only been saved by the daily delivery of tons of refuse from the neighbouring town of Lucca. The rats are apparently well-content for Lucca has a better gastronomic reputation than Pisa.

One man's garbage is another man's salvation.

Under cover of all this, that arch-commensal, town-dweller supreme, the house mouse, might have been hoping to escape being 'named', as we could say. But as far as damage is concerned, the only difference between Burns' wee, sleekit, cowerin', timorous beastie and its formidable cousin is size. The mouse is in effect a rat in miniature and is perhaps even more insidious because of its smaller size and less obtrusive ways. Wainscot, floorboards, drawers, cupboards, closets, larders, it literally has the run of many a town house, colonizing entire blocks of dwellings. And this 'wee beastie', really beautiful with its silky fur and delicate ears and large eyes,

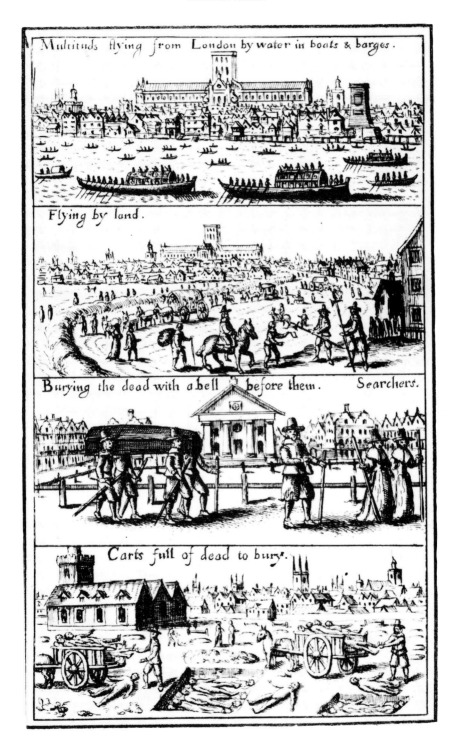

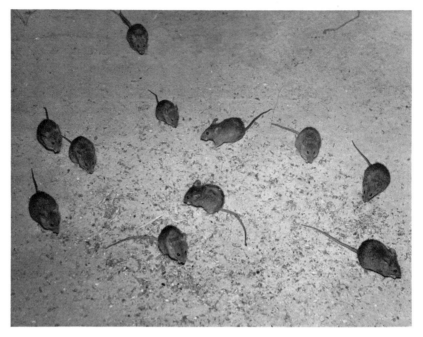

'In baiting a mouse-trap with cheese,' advised Saki, alias H. H. Munro, 'always leave room for the mouse.'

is even tougher and more adaptable than the rat. Charles Darwin showed that some mice could live 'where a drop of fresh water can never be found, excepting dew'. But they can do even without that, sometimes passing their whole existence inside a sack of flour or grain without ever quitting it. However, the most astonishing habitat house mice have been known to adopt is the refrigerated storage space used in wholesale meat depots. In these ostensibly unpropitious circumstances they verily thrive, rearing more numerous litters than normal.

'In total darkness, and in a temperature never above 15 degrees F. (about minus 10 degrees C.), with no food other than meat, the mice breed and live their entire lives,' wrote Harrison Matthews in *British Mammals*. 'They make nests of the hessian material in which meat is wrapped, or the fur and feathers from stored carcasses. Often they eat out burrows in carcasses of frozen meat and make their nests inside. Not only do the mice withstand the severe conditions, but they flourish on them to an unusual extent, so that the average size and weight of cold-store mice is above that of outside mice.'

If one can be fancifully anthropomorphic for a moment, what glee there must have been among the murine population as this humble creature came to appreciate the fundamental change taking place when man adopted a

The house mouse does not always live up to its name. The naturalist Fraser Darling described how he found considerable numbers of house-mice living on Lunga, one of the Treshnish Isles off the west coast of Scotland, even though it had been uninhabited for eighty years. However, they reverted to type straightaway, gladly colonizing his camp.

fixed abode and ceased from wandering. No longer the constant round of danger from weasel and hawk and owl and snake. No longer the ever-lasting search for food in prairie and woodland. 'Boy, oh boy,' we can imagine our spiritual progenitor of Mickey Mouse exclaiming, 'shelter and safety and warmth and food, all mod. con., all for free' and, anticipating Shakespeare,—'What a piece of work is a man!'

Apart from numbers and hardihood, a factor which makes rats and mice such a menace is their peculiar dental formation (a characteristic shared of course with other rodents). These teeth are particularly remark-able in that the incisors never stop growing. Only the front side of these incisors, of which there is a pair in both upper and lower jaws, are coated with protective enamel. The back surface is formed of softer ivory or dentine, with the result that constant work produces a very sharp chisel edge, enabling the animals to tackle extremely hard material.

But because of this characteristic continual growth in the teeth, rat and mouse—and other rodents—need the counteraction of each set of incisors to keep the other in check. Many museums contain vivid illustra-tions, in the shape of skulls, of what happens if a rodent loses one of its incisors. The tooth in the opposing jaw continues to grow unimpeded, leading eventually to death by starvation or from the unrestrained incisor piercing the brain.

Normally, however, these age-old murine commensals of man con-tinue their nefarious activities in cities and towns throughout the world, from Montreal to Moscow and from Peking to Pernambuco, gnawing their way steadily through substances as varied as lead pipes, floorboards, doors, even concrete, to get at the never-failing table spread out for them.

CHAPTER SIX

Winged Scavengers

The rat of course is both scavenger and pillager. Other wild denizens of the city have played an historic role principally as scavengers, and in the case of certain birds they were for many centuries (and still are in some towns) of immense importance in the matter of public hygiene.

As far as London was concerned, the classic case was that of the kite—which, together with other wild animals, had long appreciated that man was not only a dirty creature but also supremely wasteful. His way of life has been so wide-ranging that the by-products are almost inexhaustible, while ever-increasing human numbers produced more ordures and more waste. *Milvus milvus* flourished as a result. Even people who have never set eyes on the bird may be acquainted with Shakespeare's warning 'when the kite builds, look to lesser linen', and it is true that in making its nest the 'glead' will purloin anything in the way of scraps of clothing. But more fitting here is Hamlet's regret that he had not 'fatted all the region's kites with this slave's offal'—meaning his 'bloody, bawdy villain' of a stepfather.

For during hundreds of years the kite prospered marvellously in London, as did the raven, fellow-guest at the often sordid table of humanity, aided and abetted by carrion crow and magpie. Most gruesome of their provender was the remains of traitors whose heads were spiked on London Bridge and soon made eyeless by the fowls of the air. As the 'Twa Corbies' or ravens said to one another

> Ye'll sit on his white hause-bane [neck-bone],
> And I'll pick out his bonnie blue een.
> Wi' ane lock of his gowden hair
> We'll theek [mend] our nest when it grows bare.

Though the supply of traitors might be limited, household refuse and ordures were not. They were simply ditched in the streets and a bucket of slops on your head was a daily hazard. *Gardyloo* was a warning verily to be heeded—and 'loo' (or water) was very much a euphemism. Dead dogs and cats were commonplace and left to rot, while considerable numbers of farm animals were either brought into town or kept in surrounding paddocks and yards, the shambles where they were slaughtered being places of horror. Nothing ever came of attempts to remove city slaughterhouses to 'some remote and convenient place neere unto the river of Thames, to the

The slightly smaller black kite is seen here above a red kite. Perhaps surprisingly the kite was a favourite quarry in mediaeval hawking, its masterful flight making it a formidable target for the falcon.

end that the blood and garbige of the beasts that are killed may be washed away with the tide'. Man has been a long time solving his problems of hygiene and sanitation—he got himself into the air by means of the balloon and invented the steam locomotive before he evolved an adequate drainage system. In New York, for example, in 1840, when the city's population was already 300,000, John Rublowsky records that 'more often than not, garbage was simply tossed into the streets where roaming pigs, dogs, and chickens rooted through the piles of debris'.

So in mediaeval London, the winged scavengers such as kites and ravens were essential and in return for the vital task they performed their teeming numbers were protected with the force of law. One fifteenth-century visitor to London, secretary to the Venetian ambassador, reported that

The black kite on this Indian parapet
looks twice the size of the house crow.
But the latter is twice as cheeky
and it is he who is far more likely to
sneak in through that open door.

Nor do the people of London dislike what we abominate, that is to say crows, rooks, jackdaws; and the raven may croak at his pleasure, for no one is concerned about the omen; there is even a penalty attached to destroying them, as they say that they keep the streets of the town free from all filth. It is the same with the kites, which are so tame that they often take food from the hands of children.

But in spite of such critical words, similar scavengers evidently operated in other cities, for example, in the stews of Paris where the contemporary Francois Villon spent much of his life—

The rain has rinsed and washed us
And the sun has dried and blackened us,
Magpies and ravens have caved our eyes
And plucked out our beards and eyebrows.

76

In times when plague was a constant threat, the last great outbreak being in 1665, the aid to hygiene of these winged scavengers, however modest, was of the utmost importance. But as conditions 'improved', human gratitude to these birds abated. By the eighteenth century 'vermin-killers' were being paid for exterminating kites and ravens. By early Victorian times euphemistically named 'dust-collectors' waxed fat removing the contents of privies and the piles of decaying human excrement and ashes left in the poorer neighbourhoods, all extremely valuable as fertilizer.

So London could dispense with the winged scavengers that had for so long been commoner than starlings were at that particular time. Up to the middle of the eighteenth century the raven remained a common London bird and it was said that a town bird could easily be distinguished from a country bird by his dulled or dusty looking plumage, the result of his scavenging among 'dust' heaps. In the town of Enfield, on the northern edge of London, ravens went on nesting in a well-known 'raven-tree' until well into Victorian times. To use John Clare's words—

> Upon the collar of a huge old oak
> Year after year boys mark a curious nest
> Of twigs made up a faggot near in size
> And they to reach it try all sorts of schemes.

But in London itself the last known pair nested in Hyde Park until 1826, when 'it entered into the head of one of the park-keepers to pull down the nest containing young birds. The name and subsequent history of this injurious wretch have not been handed down,' fulminated W. H. Hudson, but expressed the hope that his soul, along with the souls of all other wanton destroyers of man's feathered fellow-creatures, was now suffering a particularly nasty fate.

Solitary ravens continued to appear in central London from time to time, including one that stole a gold bracelet fallen from a lady's wrist in Kensington Gardens. That particular bird became so notorious for its escapades that it was caught and had its wings clipped, whereupon it fell into the Serpentine and was drowned—from grief, according to popular belief, at being deprived of its powers of flight. Nowadays, apart from the traditional birds kept for symbolic reasons at the Tower of London, this magnificent, once-common town bird, subject to so much folk-lore and superstition, survives among the granite tors of Dartmoor and the hills and cliffs of Wales and Scotland. In Addis Ababa, capital of Ethiopia, its cousin, the thick-billed raven, finds plenty of scope for its garbage-hunting.

As for the kite, the last pair of London birds had nested in the gardens of Gray's Inn—perhaps casting a speculative look at the wigs of the lawyers passing below. Inverted, one of those horse-hair contraptions would have made splendid nesting material. Maybe the lawyers were apprehensive of that, for in 1777 the nest was pulled down, insult being added to injury by the young kites being dissected 'in the interests of ornithological science' to determine what they had been fed on.

As if nostalgically visiting the erstwhile haunts of its ancestors, the kite has been sighted once or twice since the war soaring over the north-eastern fringes of London, but in general it is in a precarious state in the country, though thanks to devoted work by the Royal Society for the Protection of Birds (protecting it as much against over-eager bird-watchers as against egg-thieves) its handful of numbers has slightly increased to about twenty-eight breeding pairs in the woods of North Wales, where the bird is recognizable by its buoyant flight and deeply wedged tail. (That wedged tail is a trade mark of the kites, but none is as striking as that of the well-named swallow-tailed kite of America, painted so superbly by John-James Audubon.) Incidentally, it has never been satisfactorily determined whether the kite that frequented London in such numbers was the red or the black variety. The black kite has never been known to nest in Britain; however it is a very gregarious bird—far more so than the red kite.

Though such winged scavengers have passed out of memory in the cities of the north, others are still active, even though not essential, in or around many southern cities—in France and Spain, for instance, let alone south-eastern Europe. One can frequently see assemblages of black kites doing a recce near the enormous garbage dumps outside towns such as Albi or Villeneuve, or sitting contemplatively in the surrounding trees, watching the latest delivery.

Occasionally, too, they are joined by the summer visitor, the Egyptian vulture, which comes from the African savannah to nest in the Pyrenees, but often ranges far afield in search of food. This is one of the smallest of the vultures, scarcely longer than a buzzard and much less bulky. It is striking in appearance, its wings lightly curved and pointed, the primaries black, in contrast with its white body. In the air it is a beautiful sight, with its graceful, nonchalant action and its slender silhouette. It wheels endlessly, watching, surveying, spying anything worthwhile—and keeps an eye on the movements of other birds.

For vultures hunt by sight, not smell, as was proved by 'Stupor mundi', the Emperor Frederick II, as long ago as the early thirteenth century. He carried out experiments by 'sealing' the eyes of vultures and finding that they could then in no way locate their food. Knowing the reputation of the Emperor, sealing is possibly a euphemism for more drastic methods— he once had two of his servitors cut open in his curiosity about the digestive process. But he was a great naturalist.

The controversy about vultures persisted for many years, and as late as 1830 the 'smellists', led vociferously by Charles Waterton, maintained that the birds hunted by scent. Audubon proved them wrong by painting a life-size canvas of a disembowelled sheep, which, when spread on the ground, was promptly attacked for real by nearby vultures.

As in the case of all its tribe, the appearance of the Egyptian vulture in flight is in utter contrast with its appearance on the ground when, with its bright orange-yellow, somewhat tousled head and ungainly movements, it

Audubon, the great French-American painter, shot avian specimens for his work. John Gould (b. 1804) often worked from stuffed specimens, as in the case of these Egyptian vultures.

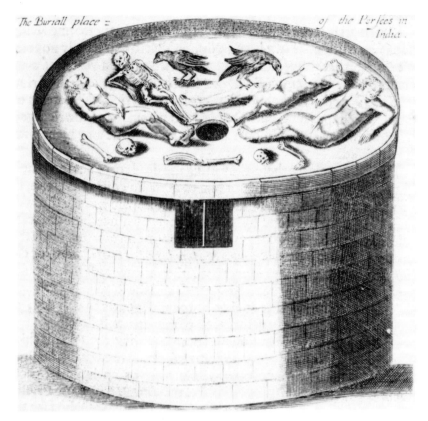

The modern Parsees believe that the souls of the dead arrive at the Bridge of the Separation, where the god Mithra judges their good and evil deeds. On this Tower of Silence winged undertakers go about their work.

looks like some weird member of the Gallinaceans, waddling among the garbage. Hudson nicely sums it up thus: 'An interesting bird is the vulture in the two strangely contrasted aspects in which he appears to us: as the loathsome feathered scavenger in the one and the sublime heavenward soarer in the other, he might serve as an emblem of man in his double nature—the gross or earthly and the angelic.'

Once I saw an Egyptian vulture perching on the crenellations of Carcassonne, in south-west France, surveying the spacious lists where perhaps its ancestors had once come to feed on the carrion that abounded in far-off times when that spectacular fortress was a scene of bloody action instead of a tourist draw-card. But rare though this scavenger is in southern European towns and their environs, it is much more common in Asia and Africa. It lives up to its name in Egypt and does regular duty in and around towns such as Cairo and Alexandria, stalking about in characteristic goose-step, picking over offal and excrement.

In India, where it can be sighted in almost every town in the land, it is known as Pharaoh's chicken or, more accurately, the white scavenger vulture. It is dwarfed, both in size and numbers, by the peacock-sized white-backed or Bengal vulture. Large gatherings of this species congregate on the edge of towns, providing ample evidence of their useful, indeed essential, role as scavengers. Any animal carcase is disposed of at incredible speed. Like dreadful old termagants at a sale, the birds, hissing and screeching, jostle and elbow their way round the feast, oblivious to any passing traffic—while another town-visitor or suburbanite, the equally large but more cowardly king vulture, waits for an unregal chance to sneak in and snatch a morsel.

One of the most bizarre tasks such vultures perform is on the so-called Towers of Silence outside certain Indian towns, principally Bombay, where the Parsees, the modern Zoroastrians, rejecting burial because the earth must not be defiled by a dead body and regarding fire as too sacred to be used for cremation, take their dead to the open roofs of these buildings, to be stripped of flesh by the avian undertakers—the bones being collected for separate disposal afterwards. In spite of this custom the Parsees are among the most highly educated Indians, their women-folk emancipated and westernized.

Probably the commonest winged scavenger in India—and not only that country's commonest raptor but also the commonest bird of prey worldwide—is the Pariah kite, Kipling's Chil, who was friendly with everyone and never failed to be in at the death. This is the selfsame black kite, *Milvus migrans*, referred to earlier in connection with France—and many other European countries from Spain to Russia, where it is a summer visitor.

In India particularly it is a regular commensal of man, and I have often seen it gliding watchfully above crowded cities such as Bangalore or Mysore, then, stooping down with supreme grace and skill, retrieve some ripe booty, dodging and twisting and banking swiftly away to avoid telephone wires and raucous house-crows alike, while the stream of human, animal and motor-traffic passes by on all sides and the Rhesus monkeys in the banyan trees lift their eyebrows at it all.

That house-crow we just mentioned is well-named. Not unlike the hoodie or grey or Royston crow of northern Europe, it is handsome in a raffish kind of way. Indeed, its scientific same of *Corvus splendens* comes from the glorious metallic sheen of its plumage. It is as familiar in the cities of India and Ceylon as pigeon or sparrow or starling in the west and depends for its livelihood on human activities even more than they do.

Like its cousins, it is omnivorous and anything from a dead sewer rat to a clutch of eggs or from peepul figs to an unwary street-vendor's chappatties is acceptable to it. Occasionally it shows willing by snapping up any stray locust, precursor perhaps of more to come, and will do a stint at a termite nest more to amuse itself than otherwise. But it is a real city gamin and likes nothing better than creeping—the only word, for it is astonishingly cunning, subtle as a shadow—into kitchen or restaurant or bedroom to filch what it can, if necessary brazening things out with an almost human insolence.

In a coastal town such as Cochin it keeps sedulous company with the fishermen plying their huge dip-nets which are worked by a heavy counter-balance of stones. In large numbers the crows perch on the 'gantries' watching speculatively as the creaking structures majestically bow down to the water. Then, immediately the cascading nets come rising up again, the feathered horde (like a mob of seagulls elsewhere) pounces on the gleaming catch, snatching up dozens of tiny fish before the fishermen can finish smoking their long bidis or chewing their betel nut.

Large flocks of house-crows gather every night in communal roosts in favourite trees along the streets or in parks or gardens, and the brief tropical dusk is loud with their raucous din as they squabble for a perch—while the monkeys, always anxious at the coming of night, believing the world still to be populated by leopards, add their protests, and the rose-ringed parakeets scream indignantly, knowing the crows as public enemies supreme. For nothing is safe from the house-crow—the only creature that at all gets its own back is the koel, a member of the cuckoo family, which lays its egg in the house-crow's nest—and then goes off yelling *kik kik kik* in triumph.

The hoodie crow can be seen prowling about cities and ports as far apart as Dublin or Tromso or Stockholm, but in more southerly cities of Europe the carrion crow, that other cousin, though now far less numerous, has for many centuries been a town-dweller. Like the house-crow, it enjoys communal roosts, even in London, at Ken Wood and Walthamstow, for example, but in the inner city it is mainly seen in places such as Hyde Park or Richmond Park or scavenging down on the Thames mud, either solitary or in pairs.

Opinions vary greatly about the crow. To many people it is a 're-morseless, treacherous, kindless villain, slayer of fledgelings, murderer of lambs, scourge of the henyard . . .' 'It is rascally . . . it indulges in knavish tricks . . . has more than the usual allowance of devilment in its make-up . . . Its mouth is full of cursing and bitterness.' Douglas St Leger-Gordon said, 'This dark ghoul of a bird has not even beauty of form or melody of song to plead his cause. His flight is laboured and ungainly, his plumage dingy, his voice harsh and proverbially unmusical . . .' E. W. Hendy: 'the raven when he swears, does it like a gentleman; his cousin's remarks recall a Thames bargee or habituée of Billingsgate.'

In contrast, W. H. Hudson, understandably conscious of the fact that any genuine wildlife in the city was to be welcomed, called it 'the grandest

Like the legendary geese of Rome,
the ravens of the Tower of London are said to
have alerted the royal forces to danger
by croaking at a band of traitors intent on
a secret take-over.

wild bird in the metropolis', far more worthwhile than exotic swans and ducks and geese that had to be fed 'bucketfuls of meal and grain to keep them going'.

There are few finer sights in the wild bird life of London than one of these crow visitors to the park on any autumn or winter morning, when he will allow you to come quite near to the leafless tree on which he is perched, to stand still and admire his massive raven-like beak and intense black plumage glossed with metallic green, as he sits flirting his wings and tail, swelling his throat to the size of a duck's egg, as at intervals, he pours out a succession of raucous caws—the cry of a true savage, and the crow's 'voice of care', as Chaucer called.

Villain though it may be in some eyes, the carrion crow is intensely interesting in itself (even St Leger-Gordon admits: 'savage, predatory, repulsive as he is, a more remarkable creature does not exist in all the wild. His worst

A nice rogues' gallery, but a more peaceful scene than it
would have been if these five species had actually
been found together: jackdaw, rook, grey crow,
magpie and raven.

enemy must fain confess him to be the wisest of birds') and also because,
delight though we may in the urban visits of swallows and swift and black
redstart and nightingale and all those others, the crow somehow evokes a
far more dramatic atmosphere, because it is a relic of those distant times
when the boundary between city and country was much less clearly defined.
The very name of 'carrion crow' has a hint of the mediaeval in it.

Whether in Europe or North America, few towns are without their
crows which nest in many a municipal park, from Wave Hill in the Bronx to
Watts Park in Southampton, often unknown or unnoticed, for no bird is
more cunning or circumspect or uncannily wary in its exits and entrances.
No shadow can slide away as unobtrusively as a crow leaving its nest. But
it is a devoted parent, often having been observed in hot weather spreading
its wings over its fledglings to protect them from the sun.

As for those other members of the corvine family, Hendy remarked that
'the rook's caw has sweet reasonableness in it compared with the note of
either crow or raven', while Gilbert White called the noise of rooks at their
evening sky-larking 'a pleasing murmur, very engaging to the imagination,

And here 'the many wintered crow' takes stock. T. A. Coward mentioned a gamekeeper observing to him that 'the Rook say "Caw", but t'other un der say "pawk, pawk". He's so fond of a bit of meat.'

Regular migration takes place among many rooks. Numbers of immigrants
reach our shores in autumn from Scandinavia and Germany.

like the rushing of the wind in tall trees, or the tumbling of the tide upon a pebbly shore'. Though some people may be irritated by it, there is something deeply evocative about the sound of a rookery, conjuring up images of the cathedral close, of 'all good people' trooping to service, while the organ murmurs on, redolent of a tranquillity now vanished for ever. Rookeries do still exist in the middle of cities such as Oxford and Bristol and Cheltenham, but in London the once large rookery in Kensington was destroyed when seven hundred trees were felled a century ago. Hudson cursed as criminals worthy of the gallows the perpetrators of such a deed that deprived Londoners of a sacred possession which had provided them with a precious touch of nature in the midst of their drab lives.

Before that act of sacrilege, rooks, it is said, could be seen together with house-sparrows, fluttering and jostling among the innumerable cabs that thronged the streets, foraging for the grain spilt from nosebags or even contained in the horse-dung. As we have said, the gradual disappearance of horse-drawn traffic played a part in reducing the sparrow population in a city such as London, and may even have affected the rooks, too, to some extent. For though the rook will spurn very little in the way of food, it is the most vegetarian of the crows, grain being one of the chief items in its diet. So, as cities spread, the species was forced to move farther out in order to be within reach of arable fields. But balancing the plunder they may sometimes wreak on cornfields, is the immense good rooks do in the number of wireworms they consume.

Being more adaptable in every way, from feeding habits to nesting sites, the jackdaw (or belfry-crow to use a nice old name for it) has been an inveterate town-dweller long before the notorious bird of Rheims which, cursed by the Cardinal for stealing his ring, eventually returned, a pitiful sight—

> His feathers all seem'd to be turn'd the wrong way;—
> His pinions droop'd—he could hardly stand—
> His head was as bald as the palm of your hand.

As far as London is concerned, the jackdaw has been an uncommon bird for a century, its main haunts now being such open spaces as Richmond Park, where it can sometimes be seen sedulously searching for tics on the backs of the deer, while a few birds still nest in Kensington Gardens, a relic of the large numbers that used to frequent them. There was certainly no lack of nesting sites, for at one time the 'ecclesiastical daw' had some sixteen hundred churches to choose from in the capital—yet only inhabited three of them at that time.

Outside London (and Rheims!) there are still many towns whose cathedrals and churches have their colonies of jackdaws and Hudson provides a pleasant angle on their presence.

I have often thought that it was due to the presence of the daw that I was ever able to get an adequate or satisfactory idea of the beauty and grandeur of some of our finest buildings. Watching the bird in his aerial evolutions, now suspended motionless, or rising and falling, then with half-closed wings precipitating himself downwards, as if demented, through vast distances, only to mount again with an exulting cry, to soar beyond the highest tower or pinnacle, and seem at that vast height no bigger than a swift in size—watching him thus, an image of the structure over and around which he disported himself so gloriously has been formed—its vastness, stability, and perfect proportions—and has remained thereafter a vivid picture in my mind. How much would be lost to the sculptured west front of Wells Cathedral, the soaring spire of Salisbury, the noble roof and towers of York Minster and of Canterbury, if the jackdaws were not there!

Indeed, the jackdaw should be an ideal avian town-dweller. Not only is it by far the most sociable of the crows, but it is one of the friendliest of all wild birds. With its grey poll, its blue irides, its merry, conversational cries and its evident enjoyment in life, it is a highly likeable character. It takes readily to human company, though it has to be admitted that the scraps put out on a hospitable window-ledge are often regarded as an open invitation to the sort of thievery that got the jackdaw of Rheims into so much trouble.

What is more, its nesting habits often cause dire distress to the householder who hasn't been prudent enough to wire his chimney-pots. Many a town chimney has been blocked by the enormous quantities of material jackdaws use, whole cartloads having to be removed at times. Similarly, at the end of the last war, when the time came to ring out the church bells in triumph after their enforced silence, one belfry was found to be so piled with four years' accumulation of corvine debris that Housman's plea 'o noisy bells be dumb' was answered in that particular parish.

E. W. Hendy, after praising the rook's voice, referred to the comic element in the 'villainous jargon' of jackdaw, magpie and jay. Comic the jackdaw does sound at times, for there is something of the natural clown in its make-up. But also, there is, to our ears at least, humour in its cries of 'tchack' and 'cae', which blend in a kind of harmony expressive of the bird's good nature.

'Villainy' perhaps applies more to magpie and jay, both to be seen on town commons and parks, even London parks such as Richmond and Regent's, but in partial mitigation of their egg-plundering and fledgling-slaughter, they are two of our most beautiful birds—the magpie with its handsome, almost porcelain-like pied plumage shot with silky blue, green and violet, and its long, graduated black tail with its sometimes bronzy-green lights—and the jay with its black-tipped crest of whitish feathers, its

If favoured habitat counts for anything, the jackdaw must be
the most religious of birds.

'moustache', its beige plumage, and its striking wing coverts which are splendidly barred with blue, black and white.

Handsome though the jay is, it is outshone by that other town visitor, the blue jay, which can be seen in the parks and suburbs of New York, Washington and other American cities. This crested, vividly blue and white member of the crow family is among the commonest birds of America, and is certainly one of the most beautiful. In common with its relations, its usual voice is harsh and strident, and it seems continually intent on identifying itself, calling out 'jay-jay'. But its mating 'song' has been called 'rather bell-like, as though two pieces of crockery were knocking together'.

Harsh indeed is the voice of the nutcracker, which occasionally visits towns in Russia—I have seen it in Sokolniki Park in Moscow, searching

The herring-gull is a more doughty rag-picker than the rook, which will clearly have to give way on this rubbish-dump. The herring-gull's cry of anger is like a rapid bark, wow, ow, ow.

for hazelnuts with its long bill, a jay-sized, chocolate-brown bird covered with large white spots. Often it gathers nuts and seeds for the winter, storing them, like some avian squirrel, in an old nest.

As a postscript, it should perhaps be added that, villains though some members of the crow family are, they all do great good through the number of injurious insects included in their diet. As the nineteenth-century French naturalist Jules Michelet said in his *L'Insecte*, 'if it were not for the birds the world would be at the mercy of the insects.'

And in city park and suburban backyard, even 'the many-wintered crow' is welcome as an example of the nature that still exists side by side with man.

CHAPTER SEVEN

A Night on the Town

There is nothing particularly fanciful about the imagined scene that leads in this chapter. The fox is one of the most notorious instances of wildlife taking up residence in town, both in Britain and America. It is also an example of the never-failing adaptability of nature.

A powdering of frost already covered the lawn as the fox emerged from the dense thicket of rhododendrons in Ken Wood. The December sky was a glowing bowl, lit not by stars but by the reflection of the surrounding metropolis. And this dull glow seemed to hum or murmur constantly, but the noise was in fact from the never-ending traffic, just as the whisper of blood never ceases. Nearer at hand the street lamps on Spaniards Road and Hampstead Lane showed up, whipped every now and then by the flash of headlights. But there were lights still closer—across the lawn some of the windows of the Georgian mansion were lit up as the security guard made his round through the famous galleries where Vermeers and Rembrandts were housed.

For once the fox seemed uncertain about its intentions, pausing with sharp muzzle questing the air and one forepaw raised as if waiting for a reassuring silence. Presently the animal trotted off delicately, leaving that unique single line of tracks, a spoor far daintier than that of any dog. For a moment it halted attentively at its accustomed gap in the palings, then bolted low-bellied across the road, glimpsed by the next late home-going driver who came sweeping round the bend.

Lithely, springily, nimble as a cat, the fox leapt over a garden wall, crossed a flower-bed, sprang on to the roof of a coal-bunker, and down into a courtyard. It was on its nightly dustbin round and, though it has to be admitted that it didn't actually know the names of the different houses, it knew intimately the places likely to yield the choicest garbage. Its technique was impeccably expert and within minutes a metal lid was clanging on the flagstones. That night the fox was in such an irresolute mood that the noise startled it. Moreover, a beslippered citizen was just then putting out the cat which, in panic at the vulpine smell, scratched its owner and bolted into the house again, though as often as not in urban encounters it is the cat which outfaces the visitor. In turn, the fox streaked back the way it had come, crossed the road so recklessly that brakes screamed as a driver instinctively tried to avoid it, to be hooted at angrily by an oncoming single-decker bus.

Inside the park again, it was a scream of a different kind that made the fox pause and listen intently. It was this that had made it so uncertain

Not an outsize household pet but a Florida alligator that has wandered into a
Miami suburb in search of water during a drought. In favourable circumstances
alligators can live up to fifty years.

in its behaviour—the mating scream of the vixen away on the grassy
slopes below the mansion. Swiftly the fox made off, through the arbour
at the side, across the lime avenue, and down into the dim light of the vast
lawns on which in daytime hundreds of people had strolled. From the lake
came the warm, tempting smell of mallard; a nervous moorhen uttered its
metallic call. But the fox was not to be distracted now. It was no longer
irresolute. It loped on purposefully in response to the vixen's call.

In the woods beyond the lake it paused alertly. Some other nocturnal
creature was on the prowl, grunting—scratching—searching. A long pied
head and silver grey body passed slowly by. It was a badger. Though they
eyed each other warily, neither animal was put out by the other's presence.
Each was intent on its own private affairs.

But the fox was now agitated about something else. A barking yap not
far away told it that another dog-fox had arrived, drawn by the same
vixen. Resentfully, the two dog-foxes circled, snarled, made a tentative
rush at each other, but swerved away circumspectly. Green eyes glaring,

In towns world-wide, foxes have realized the pickings to be had. For the
moment the ducks on the ice of Stockholm harbour seem unconcerned, but those
two foxes obviously have something in mind.

they halted to size up the situation, while the eerie scream of the vixen could be heard above the distant rumble of traffic.

Wild animals rarely fight each other in earnest. The first brush usually proves who is dominant (even among butterflies!). Life is too hazardous for them to risk an injury that might have crippling results. Even more rarely do they 'fight to the death'. Once only have I known of a case in which rival foxes had a fatal encounter. A Devon farmer was astonished one morning to come across an exhausted, dishevelled fox dragging along the dead body of another. Evidently the two animals had been fighting, and the teeth of the dead fox, in biting the neck of its rival, had met and locked under the other's hide. When the farmer found them, the surviving fox had been in the process of trying to drag itself into cover, hampered by the grim burden from which it could not escape.

There is nothing unusual about those London vulpine sorties just described. Unknown to the majority of the human city-dwellers, it is the kind of nocturnal activity taking place increasingly among the world of nature that exists in urban areas. When I used to stay at Ken Wood House, there were many occasions when the foxes could be seen; even the cubs once or twice near their den in the private part of the grounds. Once the park gates were shut and the public had departed, the place became a private domain, as it were, of which the foxes had the free run—garbage bins near at hand, the occasional duck on the lake, a surprising number of rabbits, and a plentiful supply of field-voles and rats—for the fox is a champion ratter. And, perhaps to the surprise of many people, he consumes large numbers of earthworms.

And all around, far and near, London's never-ending traffic growled and murmured and a million lights kept up their all-night radiance.

Those Ken Wood foxes were only a few among the many which frequented—and still frequent—various open spaces and parks and commons in and around London. They had an even greater freedom on nearby Hampstead Heath, while such was the vulpine population in the capital and its suburbs that the London Natural History Society found it worthwhile to conduct a survey of foxes—and they included badgers in the operation as well, so it was nicknamed the 'Brock and Tod' investigation. Badgers, incidentally, though not the inveterate scavengers that town foxes have become—nor as numerous—are virtually omnivorous, enjoying anything from flower-bulbs to carrion—and also sandwiches discarded by urban picnickers. In recent years badgers have taken to visiting suburban gardens and in some cases have actually established themselves there. One of their favourite London haunts has always been Richmond Park, where at one point not long ago there were no fewer than eight active setts.

Foxes, too, have found Richmond Park a fine haven, its open, rolling acres resembling a piece of real countryside. And Wimbledon Common, in the midst of a crowded residential area, has a population of foxes and bad-

Badgers used to be the subject of various superstitions, such as the claim that their legs on one side were longer than those on the other, to facilitate their walking round a hillside! Nowadays the Ministry of Agriculture, practising its own pet superstition, continues to gas this 'protected' species on the disputed grounds of its spreading bovine tuberculosis.

gers only a few miles from the very centre of London. Further east, along the Thames, the 180 acres of the less well-known Greenwich Park harbours cockney foxes which occasionally help themselves to wild mallard, while on one occasion a cub 'invited' the park superintendent's terrier to a game. That, as a matter of interest, is not unique. There are many instances of foxes offering to play with dogs whose owners have been taking them for a walk in the countryside.

Some foxes that have taken to urban life have set up home on railway embankments on busy commuter lines running out of London to places such as Beckenham. Train-drivers used to slow down so that their passengers could get a better view of fox-cubs playing on the grassy slopes above the track. But though the animals were safe enough from human intrusion, they weren't always safe from the trains. The London Passenger Transport Board once held an exhibition at Charing Cross station of wild animals killed on the line, including foxes, badgers and, surprisingly, otters.

The jackal frequently breeds with the pariah dogs of Indian towns.

But one vixen found a safe residence on a bomb-site bang opposite the entrance to Stockwell Underground Station, where she successfully reared her litter.

Apart from London, foxes are resident in towns as varied as Bath, Brighton, Edinburgh, Glasgow and many others. In most places they are tolerated, welcome, it might almost be said, as instances of wildlife coming to town. In some less appreciative municipalities, however, marksmen have been hired to shoot them, an unimaginative piece of Bumbledom, manifestation of man's age-old fear of the wild.

Perhaps the most remarkable and numerous vulpine city population is in Bristol, where more than two hundred litters have been recorded. The foxes live mainly on Bristol Downs, overlooking Avon Gorge and hemmed in on the other sides by the city and its suburbs. They come and go with what can only be termed nonchalance, often being seen in broad daylight strolling away from garden or parkway. One vixen actually brought up her cubs underneath the floorboards of a house; another under a church hall, the cubs coming and going through broken air-bricks, undisturbed even when choir-practice was taking place above them.

These and other intimate details of vulpine urban life were shown in a brilliant film made by the BBC. It contained astonishing night-time glimpses of the Bristol foxes at work—jumping on to bird-tables to filch the remaining crumbs—making caches of food in back gardens with other opportunist foxes promptly raiding those same caches—of an old lady calling up the local foxes for their supper—of motorists stopping to throw out food for them—and of foxes sleeping blatantly on the roofs of porches or garages.

These town foxes are not a passing phenomenon. Except for traffic— though they are developing a kerbside drill—they are safer in built-up areas than in the country where they have to contend with greedy fur-trappers, prejudiced farmers, and mindless fox-hunters. Nor are they confined to British towns. In the United States and Canada, the same red fox, which is surely one of the most beautiful of wild creatures, is nowadays a regular urban visitor, a garbage specialist likewise. In many American cities it has become a permanent resident, fox-cubs having been reared in parks and cemeteries and vacant lots in Boston and Philadelphia, to give only two examples. The most notorious case was the fox den that was found under one of the stands in the famous Yankee Stadium.

An ironical case of the fox becoming an urban resident is in Brisbane. The species was introduced into Australia during the nineteenth century, in the hope that it would combat the plague of rabbits which had increased from the original three pairs let loose in New South Wales. But the fox didn't do his stuff at the time (any more than stoat and weasel, other anti-rabbit introductions). But perhaps nowadays those Brisbane foxes are making amends and following the rabbits and hares which have taken to visiting the local precincts.

But though an animal as adaptable as the fox is well able to establish itself, a more surprising urban invader in America is the coyote. Though much smaller than its cousin the wolf, it is still a sizeable animal, weighing around forty pounds and, from muzzle to tail-tip, measuring four feet. Its other name of prairie wolf gives an indication of its normal habitat, formerly chiefly on the western plains, though it has progressively extended

At the edge of Harar, second city of Ethiopia, spotted hyenas squabble over the day's ordures. It used anciently to be believed that the hyena 'changeth sex, being one year a male, another year a female'—Edward Topsell, *Historie of Four-footed Beasts*, *c.* 1620.

its range. For long it was persecuted by cattle-ranchers who accused it of widespread calf-slaughter. Ironically, after the resultant campaign to reduce its numbers, it was seen that the only creature to benefit was the prairie dog (a species of marmot) which, without the natural check of its main predator, the coyote, was multiplying to such an extent as to deprive those same calves of their pasture.

Nowadays in the United States the coyote is tending increasingly to venture into suburban areas and it has been reported as taking up residence in places as unlikely as Chicago and Detroit and Denver and other cities.

But if the fox is a relative newcomer to town life, the jackal is a long established urbanite. Close cousin of the fox, it is little if at all bigger, its tail is not as splendid as the fox's brush, while its general colour is a dingy grey backed with a faintly yellowish tinge. In the countryside of Africa and India it will gather in packs, its wailing cry weird and unnerving. It will hunt small creatures incapable of defending themselves, but above all it prefers carrion, often left over from lion or tiger kill, for which it competes with the vultures. In India it used to be believed that the jackal would act as a scout for the prowling tiger, uttering a special call on scenting prey, terrifying to the jungle creatures because of its significance.

In the neighbourhood of Indian towns it operates, necessarily, on its own, or in pairs, skulking among the gardens and alleyways and chicken-runs and middens, lost among the teeming multitude of humanity. I once saw one scuttle away through the bazaar area of Mysore, with a lump of meat in its mouth, and somehow survive its way through the traffic.

Some authorities in the past have claimed that the jackal was the most likely precursor of the domestic dog, having originally struck up a partnership with primitive man because of its scavenging propensities—and also perhaps acting as a game-scout for man (as for the tiger!) when he went hunting animals too big for the jackal itself to tackle. Certainly the jackal is very much at home in the company of men, but though nobody minds its scavenging activities, its liability to carry rabies among the all-too-numerous pi-dogs of eastern towns makes it less welcome.

No relation to the family Canidae, but sharing a taste for scavenging, the hyena nowadays has largely been driven out of town, though the striped hyena still occasionally ventures into the 'suburbs' of towns on the Indian Deccan. This species is almost entirely a carrion-eater, and in the sprawling, noisome Indian townships it has plenty of scope, though its numbers have been greatly reduced. The spotted hyena of Africa is also a scavenger where the opportunity arises, but is a ruthless killer in its own right, hunting in packs for young wildebeest, goats, cattle, and so on, but is no town visitor.

The hyena in general has always been looked upon with disfavour, partly because of its habits and equally uncomely appearance, for its sloping back, massive head, and powerful jaws disqualify it for any beauty contest, while its maniacal laughter is one of the most chilling sounds in nature. The conventional idea of it is summed up in Philip Gosse's description in *The Romance of Natural History*.

> With bristling mane and grinning teeth, the obscene monster glares at you, and warns you to secure a timely retreat. Another appears, bearing in its jaws a loathsome human skull and you shudder as you hear the bones crack and grind between the powerful teeth, and gladly shrink away from the repulsive vicinity.

Libellous words, perhaps, for with the right approach another side of the 'jaccatray's' character can be brought out. A few years ago in Addis Ababa, a young Ethiopian slum-dweller, sleeping rough every night in the city centre, gradually won the confidence of a street-prowling hyena which eventually would come to his call and take food from his hand.

But unexpected city-visitors are not confined to the Orient. Perhaps the most bizarre were the Florida alligators which at one time, because of habitat-encroachment, were moving into Miami in appreciable numbers, often being found in swimming-pools or on golf-courses, in backyards and even on street-corners, subjects for shaggy dog stories if you like. Police and game-wardens were kept busy rescuing alligators and returning them to the Everglades.

Even more daunting, however, are the polar bears which have taken to combing the garbage-dumps in various sub-arctic Canadian townships— to such an extent that in one case the local trade unions have had to 'bus' their members to work to avoid encountering these often aggressive, half-ton scavengers. Nansen frequently had trouble with polar bears scavenging round the ice-locked *Fram* during his famous drift—but that after all was in the desolate Kara Sea!

Seton Gordon once recorded a family of kestrels consuming ten thousand rodents in seven months.

'The grave's a fine and private place,' wrote Andrew Marvell, a sentiment that might be echoed by the many wild creatures which make their homes in churchyards and cemeteries.

In the shadow of West Thurrock Power Station, mute swans prospect for a nesting site. The name 'mute' is not exactly correct, for the bird, especially when guarding the nest, utters a defiant, explosive, almost trumpeting grunt and also hisses angrily. The nineteenth-century naturalist Yarrell spoke of its mating 'song' as being a 'soft low voice'.

CHAPTER EIGHT

Forests of the Night

Although the fox is so prominent among 'city' fauna, several other mammals usually associated with wilder haunts have begun to appreciate the advantages of urban prowling. Few people realize their presence, for they emerge only in 'the forests of the night' in public park or private garden.

In America, for example, one such mammal is the pretty racoon, a member of the family Procyonidae, to which the pandas also belong. Chunkier than a fox but about the same size, it has a handsome, ringed tail, and a masklike dark band across its face and eyes. It is an expert climber and will take birds and eggs, but prefers aquatic prey such as frogs and fish and, favourite food of all, crayfish. These it catches at the edge of stream or pond, as it rarely swims, and it has the fastidious habit of washing its food in the water, holding it in its long, slender 'fingers' and dunking it.

As a fur-bearing animal the racoon has been famous in America since the days of the legendary Davy Crockett and in the trade its fur used to be known as Alaska bear or Alaska sable, but its flesh is highly edible, too, pioneers frequently hunting it for that purpose. But in spite of its relatively small size, the racoon has always been renowned for its courage and ferocity when attacked and there are many instances of its fighting off two or three hunting-dogs.

Recently the racoon seems to have opted for a more peaceful existence, coming to the conclusion that it is safer in urban areas where there is no hunting. There is food to hand also, for it has added garbage-scavenging to its activities. Although now common in some cities, its presence is more often realized because of its tracks in mud or snow, for it is rarely sighted. But the presence of another urban newcomer can readily be ascertained through quite different means.

This is the skunk, which, with its broad white stripe along its thick, rough fur, and its jaunty, bushy tail, is a truly handsome animal. But handsome is as handsome does and its method of defence consists of squirting out a ghastly, penetrating, amber-coloured fluid from its anal glands. Anyone getting a dose of this on his clothes while chasing off the intruder might as well give them away. No dry-cleaner can help once a skunk has used its spray.

It is said that the climate of America is becoming warmer, which has probably contributed to the territorial spread of a mammal not only one of the most interesting urban invaders but one of the most interesting of mammals in general. This is the American or Virginian opossum, which,

The female racoon has up to six cubs in a litter, which remain with her for twelve-months, and family groups often sleep together. Few animals are so adept at concealing themselves as the racoon, but this is offset by its extreme inquisitiveness.

apart from one or two other members of the same family, the Didelphidae, in South America, is the only marsupial outside Australia and New Guinea. The marsupials are among nature's most primitive phenomena, the best-known being the kangaroo. Most mammals are placental, the embryo growing and forming in the mother's womb, the young creature at birth being comparatively well developed. But in the marsupials the baby is disproportionately tiny and unformed, sometimes scarcely the size of a bumble-bee even in the case of the biggest species. At birth it crawls into the pouch on the mother's belly and is even too feeble to suck for itself, the milk being fed into its mouth by means of a muscular device in the mother's teat.

Nowadays the Virginian opossum is a frequent visitor to American parks and gardens and its presence has occasionally been betrayed by its getting involved in violent confrontation with neighbourhood alley-cats. This American species has given its name to the expression 'playing possum', in other words feigning death when attacked, in the hope of being left alone. Often this ruse succeeds, leaving the opossum free to resume its inspection of neighbourhood poultry-runs.

In the Australian cities of Sydney and Melbourne, another opossum, but belonging to the family of Phalangers, has invaded private residences in considerable numbers, damaging plants and even getting into lofts of houses where it sometimes rips up the ceilings in setting up home. This is the common brush-tailed possum, otherwise known as the vulpine opossum because of its foxlike head—while it is also about the size of a fox. The Virginian opossum has several young at a time and when they are too big to be accommodated in their mother's pouch they ride around on her back. But the brush-tail female gives birth to only one baby at a time, which is perhaps fortunate as the species is now a persistent town visitor.

It is, however, far from being the only town-visiting marsupial of Australia. Other opossums, such as the mountain and ring-tailed varieties, visit the gardens of tropical Brisbane, while in addition the strange, rabbit-sized long-nosed bandicoot gets into trouble for digging up lawns. Reminiscent of the racoon's hygienic ways, it has the fastidious habit of drawing through its 'fingers' the earthworms it catches in order to clean them before eating them. Its method with mice, which it also catches, is somewhat different. It stamps them into a palatable mess first.

In the neighbourhood of places such as Mt Coot-Tha Park, a regular visitor is the 'cuddly', so-called teddy bear (it's no bear), the koala, seeking its favourite eucalyptus trees. Perhaps, too, it feels safer as a suburbanite—for until it was protected this national emblem of Australia was in danger of extinction, millions of koalas being slaughtered for their skins. You can sometimes hear the male koalas braying at night; less likely to be heard or seen is the Echidna—alias spiny ant-eater—and also the duck-billed platypus, those freaks of nature which also visit or hide up in the Brisbane suburbs.

These Monotremes or egg-laying mammals are unique in nature and there is a certain irony in these most primitive creatures—redolent of the dawn of time when nature started her experimenting—going their humble way amidst all the sophisticated world of man, with its television and motor-cars and elaborate gadgetry that he finds essential to his well-being.

Reverting to America, the most interesting mammal venturing into suburban areas is the Texas armadillo, also known as the nine-banded armadillo or Peba. The armadillos are unique among mammals because of the armour that gives them their name. This consists of bony plates in the skin which, while protecting the entire upper parts of the body, are made up of movable bands of scales flexible enough to allow the animal to roll up in a ball for self-defence.

The armadillo is one of the Edentates—mammals that are either completely toothless or possessing teeth that are virtually useless. However, nature has compensated for this by providing the armadillo with a long, extensile tongue for gathering ants and termites and it also enjoys other insects and snails. All this might make it a welcome visitor to the suburban garden were it not for its chief means of escape—which is to burrow into the earth with unbelievable rapidity. An equation would have to be worked out between the vast number of insects consumed and a ruined lawn or rose-bed.

On a smaller scale, physically but not numerically, there is no lack of mammals who have come to dwell in the 'city'. Of course, one could speculate whether they haven't always been there: generation after

These three-month-old baby opossums are only two of a litter of possibly eighteen. After ten weeks in their mother's pouch, they ride on her back.

The American or grey squirrel was first introduced into Britain in 1876.
A single pair was kept in a cage near Macclesfield in Cheshire until their owner,
tiring of them, turned them into the nearby woods. There, with typical
fortitude, they prospered.

generation of humble creatures going their secret, largely nocturnal way in
garden and backyard and municipal park and golf-course and town common and rubbish dump and pond and canal, forming, together with all
the other even less significant creatures and the abounding plant-life, an
ecology of their own in the midst of the glare and cacophony and unaware-
ness of human life that surrounds them.

Because of their discreet habits and their small size, some of the mammals in question are usually seen only by chance—or through much
patience on the part of townsfolk who have come to realize, let's say, that

a colony of water-voles is trafficking among the loosestrife of the local canal, or that the mysterious little round holes on the lawn are not necessarily the work of a mole but may have been caused by a hedgehog—for in its search for beetles and grubs, the hedgehogs will dig small, very shallow cavities, the size of a tenpence piece, sometimes a dozen or twenty in a night, a fact appreciated two hundred years ago by Gilbert White, though he was actually under the impression the animal was kindly nibbling away the roots of the troublesome plantain.

Some small mammals in town areas are unfortunately only seen when they are dead, flattened bloodily by that worst of urban predators, the automobile, as they scurry across a road. Hedgehogs have always been the worst sufferers in this respect owing to their defensive habit of rolling into a ball at the approach of danger. Interestingly in this respect it has been claimed by some naturalists that it is becoming common for the modern hedgehog to *run* out of danger on the road, instead of adopting its usual practice, which if true would be another example of nature's adaptability (cf. the town-fox's kerbside drill!).

Some small mammals are found dead in garden or common through natural causes. This is particularly so in the case of the shrew. It used to be thought that this long-nosed, irascible, aggressive little animal (which can sometimes be heard hissing and twittering in bank or border) was liable to die of shock. But one reason why its tiny carcase is found so comparatively often may be that it is more likely to die in the open, whereas mice and voles tend to pass their dying moments in burrow or ditch. In addition, not all predators like the musky flavour of the shrew's flesh and may kill the shrew without consuming it. In any case, the life-span of such 'small deer' is probably only about fifteen months and their casualties are enormous.

But because of the large numbers of insects consumed by shrews, their presence should be welcomed by every gardener—far more than that of the controversial mole, splendid engineer though he is, with those splayed, rigid, shovel-like forepaws which enable him to 'swim', as it were, through the soil, to the fury of horticulturalist and greenkeeper alike. Various shrews contend for the title of tiniest town-dwelling mammal—the least shrew of America perhaps winning by a whisker over the pigmy shrew of Europe which is a whole $2\frac{3}{4}$ inches in length, its tail adding another inch.

In the past the shrew was regarded with grave superstition, being 'of so baneful and deleterious a nature, that wherever it creeps over a beast, be it horse, cow, or sheep, the suffering animal is afflicted with cruel anguish, and threatened with the loss of the use of the limb'. Thus Gilbert White, again, and he went on to describe the brutal remedy that used to be adopted. 'Against this accident, to which they were continually liable, our provident fore-fathers always kept a shrew-ash (a tree looked upon with no small veneration), which, when once medicated, would maintain its virtue for ever. A shrew-ash was made thus:— into the body of the tree a deep hole was bored with an auger, and a poor devoted shrew-mouse was thrust in alive, and plugged in, with several quaint incantations long since forgotten.'

For long a famous 'shrew-ash' stood in Richmond Park, but was progressively demolished by time and storm so that only a vestige remains. Darwin's contemporary, Sir Richard Owen, recorded that the tree had continued to be so venerated that he knew of mothers bringing their sick children to it in the hope of a cure at the hands of certain women who knew the proper incantations and the magic time for the ceremony.

One of the largest of the family can occasionally be seen operating in some wasteland stream. This is the water-shrew, nearly six inches in length if you count its tail. As its name implies, it is aquatic in its habits and always has a favourite diving-board in the form of a stone, from which it takes little headers into the stream, where it hunts water-insects and small crustaceans and snails. Once in the water it looks exceedingly beautiful, almost fairy-like, for in its dense, velvety fur there remain pockets of air which give the animal a silvery appearance—while at the same time increasing its buoyancy.

Probably the small mammal of whose existence the townsman is most aware is the ubiquitous squirrel—the grey squirrel, needless to say, for only in a few parts of the British Isles does the native red squirrel still exist and probably not at all in any sizeable town. The grey squirrel is usually blamed for the radical decrease in the population of the red, but the fact is that the latter was already in decline, partly through disease, when the grey was introduced, notably by the Duke of Bedford at Woburn.

The grey squirrel is what might platitudinously be dubbed a loveable rogue: nothing can be prettier than a squirrel nibbling away at a nut held in its forepaws or racing up and down a tree trunk, peering round the corner with its bright eyes, flicking its bushy tail, and cursing quietly; but a more jaundiced view will be taken of it by anyone whose strawberries it has eaten or peas it has ravaged, while many a wild bird has lost eggs or fledgelings to it.

Introduced from America during the last century, the grey squirrel is yet another example of a natural species battening gleefully on to a new, ideal habitat. Before the First World War the grey squirrel was so welcome in its new home ('eminently suitable for townlife,' it was said) that in London's Hyde Park, for example, the authorities put up special notices to the effect that 'the public are earnestly requested not to molest the grey squirrels'. Forty years later other park authorities were forced to destroy four thousand grey squirrels in Kew Gardens alone, and the species was 'banned' from all the royal parks, a *diktat* at which *Sciurus carolinensis* has cocked a snook.

Grey and red squirrels can be seen often enough in daytime. A more

As many householders know, the hedgehog has a great liking for milk. But the allegations of its sometimes sucking the teats of cows is an ancient superstition without foundation—comparable with claims that it carries away apples on its spines.

nocturnal member of the sciurine family is the American flying squirrel which frequents many of the parks in New York and other American cities. It is a pity it is so retiring, for it is one of the most attractive animals in general, not merely among the squirrels. All squirrels can leap daringly from branch to branch but the flying squirrel can cover distances of twenty or thirty yards. It does not actually fly (the bat being the only mammal possessed of the power of true flight), but glides or volplanes most gracefully, perforce always in a downward plane.

This is made possible by the extensive flap of skin on either side of its body between the front and back paws. As the squirrel launches into the air, the membrane is stretched out in a sort of lateral parachute effect, while the long furry tail acts as a rudder. The similar European flying squirrel also occasionally visits parks in Finnish towns such as Savonlinna or Kuopio.

Like the reds and the greys, the flying squirrel doesn't hibernate, but in a very cold spell several of them will sensibly huddle together for mutual comfort in some hollow tree or even in one of their old and quite bulky nests.

Unrelated to but reminiscent of the flying squirrels is the marsupial sugar glider, an exceedingly pretty, soft-furred, grey and white phalanger. It visits Eastern Australian gardens more frequently than is realized, its large, innocent-looking eyes revealing its nocturnal habits. Its favourite food is the well-known 'witchetty grubs', the larvae of longicorn beetles, but it can glide up to sixty yards among the tree-tops where it catches many roosting small birds such as the tiny honey-eater. But the bloodbird, as it is sometimes called because of its brilliant red colouring, is in turn often avenged by the formidable masked owl (relation of the barn owl), which comes marauding silently through the night.

The stoat is supremely agile. In its characteristic bounding gait it can cover twenty inches at a time. It has been known to make a long jump of eight feet and spring vertically three feet into the air.

CHAPTER NINE

The Killers

We have seen in earlier chapters how large numbers of small animals exist in the cities of the world, so it is natural that various predators profit by this. Nature always fashions her own balance, rough at times though this may be. But the balance is only too easily destroyed by man.

In the past a comparatively common predator in towns and their environs was the polecat. In Elizabethan London, for instance, a well-known street-cry was that of the vermin-catcher, who never feared redundancy: 'Rats or mice! Ha' ye any rats, mice, polecats or weasels? Or ha' ye any old sows sick of the measels? I can kill them, and I can kill moles, and I can kill vermin that creepeth up and creepeth down and peepeth into holes.'

Even if it was not yet appreciated how great a part rats played in spreading the plague, they were otherwise such a menace that it was short-sighted to include some of their natural enemies in the list of 'nuisances'. After all, kite and raven were not innocent of poultry-snatching, yet they were protected with the force of law because of their usefulness as sanitary officers.

Of course the polecat is capable of killing anything from hare to wildfowl and stealing eggs, but if it gets among a rat colony, massacre ensues. Blackish-brown in colour, with a subtle purple sheen, and some whitish markings, it is very little smaller than the nowadays better known but alien mink—weighing around three pounds and measuring some $2\frac{1}{4}$ feet in length. Though it is now a rare animal in Britain, its name has been perpetuated through one of its characteristics, for 'to stink like a polecat' is only too true in fact. By means of its anal glands it can emit, as a form of defence, a mephitic odour probably only excelled by the skunk or the grass-snake, and from which it earns its other name of foumart or foulmarten.

The last polecat to be killed in the neighbourhood of London was shot on Wimbledon Common in 1939, though this could have been an escape: during the centuries large numbers of ferrets (never more than partly domesticated) have escaped from captivity, many of them breeding with wild polecats. But though the 'fitchew' has been run out of town, it might be mentioned here that there are slight signs of the polecat increasing in general.

Although some killers may have moved into town, others have stayed on. Two of these are the polecat's own close cousins, the stoat and the

weasel. Even in London, they both exist, in places such as Ken Wood*
and Hampstead, Richmond Park and on Wimbledon Common, while
town commons and parks frequently provide shelter for them, and I have
seen both species at rubbish-dumps outside French towns where the rodent
population is ever-present.

Chestnut-brown with creamy white underparts, slim, lithe, agile, the
stoat is a foot-long, splendidly neat animal, progressing normally in typical
undulating movements, but like quicksilver when necessary. It is a champion ratter, killing with a skilled and enthusiastic ruthlessness. Its ferocity is
matched by its courage, exemplified in a fight between a stoat and a much
heavier and bigger ferret, witnessed by Howard Lancum—

> and a very sanguinary affair it was. For sheer, unbridled savagery it
> could scarcely be surpassed. This battle was one of those occasions that
> are seen perhaps once in a lifetime. A friend was in the act of putting a
> ferret into a rabbit bury, and wishing to have both hands free to remove
> some undergrowth, put down the ferret for a moment on a heap of
> dead leaves. One can only surmise that the stoat had been sleeping or
> hiding under the leaves, but in a few seconds there was such a flurry of
> reddish brown and white fur that human intervention was impossible.
> In the outcome, victory was with the much bigger, domesticated
> animal, but it was a very sick ferret for a week afterwards.

The weasel is, near enough, a smaller replica of the stoat, scarcely the
span of a man's hand in length, and a lighter red in general colouring—it
also lacks the black tail tip of the stoat. It, too, is the essence of courage,
ferocity and agility, a bloodthirsty little atom, and though it will tackle
rats and rabbits at times, its usual prey is the smaller rodents and it is an
incomparable mouser. Perhaps its numbers in town areas could increase,
but in the countryside prejudice and ignorance and the selfishness of
shooting interests have caused the wholesale decline of both stoat and
weasel, whose dried-up carcases too often sadly decorate the woods and
copses. In the words of Edward Thomas,

> There was a weasel lived in the sun
> With all his family,
> Till a keeper shot him with his gun
> And hung him up on a tree,
> Where he swings in the wind and rain,
> In the sun and in the snow,
> Without pleasure, without pain,
> On the dead oak tree bough.

*Hudson, as we have seen, referred to Ken Wood as Caen Wood. A sixteenth-century variation of the
name was Cane Wood. Could this possibly derive from an old English name for the weasel: cane—a
word which in fact Gilbert White used?

The true origins of the domestic cat are still a mystery, but remains of the European wild cat have been found in caves dating back to the days of Palaeolithic man.

I suppose it would be too much to expect the polecat to be welcome in urban areas nowadays, but what a boon the weasel would be in places infested by rodents. There are many towns where it could be profitably encouraged. In Canada the much bigger long-tailed weasel occasionally visits town gardens or lots, while that other larger member of the Mustelidae, the mink, has started to prospect—perhaps interested in the muskrats which are now regular urban visitors in some North American towns. In Britain, the mink, now an established feral species originating from escapes from fur farms, is so prolific, adaptable and widespread, it would not be surprising to hear of its appearance in municipal parks, attracted by the wildfowl on ornamental lakes.

In connection with urban foxes, we mentioned that they accounted for many rats and field-voles, for they are 'killers' as well as scavengers. As far as field-voles are concerned, favourite vulpine hunting-grounds are sewage 'farms' and treatment works near large towns, such as Beddington which serves much of London. The lush herbage round such places provides a considerable food-base for wildlife, including enormous numbers of the short-tailed vole (or short-tailed field-mouse, as it is sometimes known).

Other killers beside the fox have long appreciated this, the kestrel especially having taken up residence in force at Beddington, nesting there regularly. The adaptability of the kestrel has been vividly illustrated by the large numbers that 'work' the motorway verges undisturbed by the traffic that gadarenes along without cease, while as for town-dwelling, they have nested, for example, on various unlikely sites, such as the gasworks at Bromley-by-Bow and on the power station at Greenwich, using nearby allotments as their hunting-grounds. But they have also moved into the very heart of London, where they are probably commoner than people realize. They have nested frequently in such central parts as Westminster Abbey, the Houses of Parliament, the Imperial Institute in South Kensington, and even on the Langham, part of the BBC complex.

Their hunting-grounds are the spacious parks—St James's, Green Park, Hyde Park, Regent's Park. But their favourite metropolitan beat is Richmond Park, one survey a few years ago showing there were twenty pairs with their own separate territories and it was estimated that fifty-four young birds were successfully brought off.

The hovering of the kestrel—it is the only bird that can truly hover, though others try—is one of the finest sights in nature, and the heart of any townsman should be uplifted if he is lucky enough to see it, even though the implications are violent death for some small creature. With quivering wings and wide-spread, depressed tail, the 'wind-hover' hangs in mid-air, maybe forty feet up, scrutinizing the ground below, sliding on a little way if it draws blank, hovering again—and then pouncing headlong.

Gerard Manley Hopkins evoked some of the magic of this skilled, winnowing, effortless action when he wrote

> I caught this morning morning's minion, king-
>   dom of daylight's dauphin, dapple-dawn-drawn Falcon, in his riding
> Of the rolling level underneath him steady air, and striding
>   High there, how he rung upon the rein of a wimpling wing
> In his ecstasy! then off, off forth on swing
>   As a skate's heel sweeps smooth on a bow-bend, the hurl and gliding
> Rebuffed the big wind. My heart in hiding
>   Stirred for a bird—the achieve of, the mastery of the thing!

But though hovering is the characteristic hunting action of the kestrel and small rodents such as the field-vole its chief prey, in London it has adapted itself to a more numerous prey—the house-sparrow, which it will hunt down with a dash reminiscent of the sparrowhawk. And in its own way, the flight of the sparrowhawk is as dramatic as that of any raptor. A miniature goshawk, as it were, it 'prowls' low above the ground, under cover of hedge or trees, then goes hurtling with fearful verve after its prey, blackbird or finch or robin, a pile of bloody feathers often evidence of its passing. It has frequently been seen in action on Southampton Common, for example, surrounded on all sides by streets and houses, while in London it nests regularly on Wimbledon Common and again, almost inevitably, Richmond Park. (The American sparrowhawk is a regular New York visitor, but in spite of its confusing name it is more closely related to the kestrel, its habits being similar.)

Of all the winged hunters to be seen, albeit only occasionally, in towns and cities, the peregrine falcon—formerly known as the duck-hawk in America—is the most spectacular. Cruising leisurely, high up, patiently watching—then, marking out its prey, it tips over, head first, and with wings curving back about its tail, 'stoops' with awe-inspiring speed, which, in a short attacking flight can reach nearly two hundred miles an hour.

In Britain in general the chances of seeing a peregrine are all too rare. The species has been shamefully persecuted by all and sundry, from the human jackals called egg-collectors to the Air Ministry which slew hundreds of birds during the last war, allegedly to protect their carrier-pigeons (though ironically since then peregrine falcons have often been employed at air stations to disperse the huge congregations of seagulls and lapwings). So in town areas the chances are smaller still. Nevertheless, peregrines have often been recorded as hunting pigeons over Smithfield Market and round the Tower of London, while for a hundred years there have been periodical records of birds visiting St Paul's Cathedral. At Vincennes on the northern outskirts of Paris, where Henry V died, I have several times watched falcons hunting the pigeons that nest on the ledges of Charles V's great chapel, the smack of the killing-blow, which sounds like a fist striking the palm of a hand, audible above the buzz of tourists in the courtyard. And in North American cities, peregrines have often taken to patrolling the towering ranges of the skyscrapers, living on feral pigeons again, and they still nest in places such as Manhattan.

Perhaps, paradoxically, this magnificent bird will gradually find a refuge among the concrete peaks and eyries of the city, safer amid the close company of man than along the coasts or on the moorlands where it has been so vulnerable. Nothing is more majestical than 'a falcon, towering in her pride of place'.

It cannot be pretended that there are everyday chances of seeing these various raptors in town areas, though there is a somewhat greater likelihood in the case of the kestrel. But their very unusualness would startle the eye if occasion arose. With the owls, those other winged hunters which have taken up residence in city and town and suburb, there is even less chance of their being seen, except for the occasional shadowy presence, briefly glimpsed in the aura of street-lamp or headlight. This is indeed a pity, for owls in general are superbly beautiful and interesting creatures, mysterious wanderers of the night that still disturbs us, and usually it is only their sepulchral voices we hear.

However, without ever hearing or seeing an owl, the town dweller may find other indications of its presence in park or on common or even in some suburban gardens. Unlike the hawks and falcons, owls do not skin or tear their prey. They swallow it whole, subsequently disgorging the indigestible parts in so-called pellets, neat little packages the size of a walnut. In one investigation, 700 owl pellets were examined and found to contain the remains of more than 2500 mice. It was calculated that five pairs of barn owls in a square mile of countryside (alas! you wouldn't get that incidence nowadays) were consuming close on 24,000 rats, mice and other rodents a year.

But owls may sometimes make their presence known by other methods, too. In nesting time the tawny owl can be distinctly aggressive to human intrusion. Many a nosey-parker, myself included, has received a doughty buffet on the head for prying into an owl's domestic affairs. The barn owl, as we have already mentioned, sometimes betrays its presence by 'snoring'; at least, its fledgelings do as they create a bizarre shindy in belfry or loft waiting for their parents to bring them food.

Though both barn owl and tawny owl occur in such London environs as Hampton Court Park and Richmond Park and the outlying Epping Forest, the owl most likely to be seen in English town areas, if people can recognize its rather erratic flight and mewing cry, is the little owl. For this species hunts both by day and by night, taking not only mice and shrews, but many beetles and even earthworms. This truly 'little' owl—it is scarcely bigger than a song-thrush—is alien to Britain, having been first introduced by Charles Waterton, who released a few pairs on his Yorkshire estate around 1840. This experiment failed, but after subsequent releases by Lord Lilford and others, the little owl spread rapidly over many parts of the country. Nowadays it has become an established townee, breeding in many public parks and commons.

Another species, the ground-nesting short-eared owl, can sometimes be seen in daylight, too, especially near that always profitable avian hunting-ground, the sewage farm, because of those same universal providers, the field-voles. This owl is intimately linked with those teeming rodents, and in a so-called 'plague' year when the vole population explodes, the numbers of short-eared owls increase correspondingly—just as in the Arctic the periodical irruptions of the lemmings cause their various predators to flourish.

Very different from the sewage farms are the airfields used as hunting-grounds by the snowy owl, that imposing and beautiful bird of the Arctic. For example, on the Toronto International Airport in Canada, snowy owls had regularly to be shot because of danger to aircraft, into whose jets they were occasionally sucked. Fortunately a bird-loving pilot persuaded the authorities to catch the birds instead and have them transferred to safer regions. The same practice has, incidentally, been adopted there in connection with red-tailed hawks, which also found good hunting on the

The kestrel does not make a nest in the true sense. A ledge in a church tower is home enough for its squealing young ones, though at times it will adopt the abandoned nest of another species, such as the carrion crow.

wide acres of the landing-ground. Several dozen of both species are rescued from the airport every year.

Two owls that are from time to time recorded as winter visitors in some American towns, including New York, are the barred owl, similar to the European tawny, and the long-eared owl, while a long-established resident, breeding in parks and gardens is the attractive, puckish, tufty-eared little screech owl, whose pleasant call belies its name.

One small avian killer, totally unlike the owls or hawks, is the red-backed shrike, which very occasionally breeds in urban areas of Britain, to which it is a late and brief summer visitor. Related to the minivets which frequent Indian gardens, the 'butcher-bird' is a ferocious little predator—and a handsome one, too, with its French-grey head, reddish-brown wings and dull white breast tinted with a delicate rose. A thick, black moustache-like streak across the sides of the head helps to increase its 'fierce' look.

The shrike waits in ambush on some convenient fence post and then dashes out with great verve after bumble-bee and cockchafer and will even take fledgelings and young mice, seizing them in its slightly hooked beak. These it impales on the spikes of blackthorn or hawthorn or barbed wire, a handy larder for future reference—and possibly for the use of its own young when they leave the nest.

To lift a phrase from a different context—the barn owl 'for gain not glory, winged his roving flight'. On those lovely wings the species occasionally travels long distances. One young bird ringed in Dumfries was later recovered near Grantham in Lincolnshire, 210 miles away.

A killer that deserves a thumbnail to itself is, perhaps to the surprise of some people, the cat. Now, very often the term 'wild cat' is used loosely and inaccurately: the true wild cat, *Felis sylvestris*, is a thickly built, thickly furred animal, with strong black striping on its sides and black bands on its thick, short tail. Somewhat grandiloquently, the eighteenth-century naturalist Thomas Pennant dubbed it the British tiger. Fierce, solitary, perhaps ten or eleven pounds in weight, it inhabits the glens of Scotland and parts of south-eastern Europe, preying on hares and grouse, the occasional lamb, and is capable of taking a roe-deer fawn.

But the 'wild cat' of common parlance is the domestic cat gone wild, the feral cat in other words. In all the cities of the world, especially large metropolises such as New York, London, Paris, Rome, a staggering population of feral cats exists, animals whose origins in some cases stem back many feline generations. Secretive to a degree, highly nocturnal, savage in danger, unseen and unknown by the vast majority of people, they have gone wild through various causes—war, fire, floods, and other factors that have displaced their erstwhile owners. But the chief cause is that 'I love little pussy, her coat is so warm', too often becomes a different tune when the sweet little kitten inconveniently grows up and is booted out of doors.

And so, for one reason or another, the numbers of these feral cats increase year by year. Many of them by now are really wild, never having known a human home. The wild instincts dormant or atrophied in the hearthside pet come to the surface again and these cats to all intents and purposes lead a completely wild existence in the concrete jungles they inhabit, breeding in warehouse and sewer and factory and ruined building. The legendary independence of the domestic cat is just not true—it may have a disdainful manner, but it still comes for its saucer of milk, its bowl of catfood, its place on the armchair. But the feral cat is totally independent, totally self-reliant, every bit as committed a hunter as its wild kin in the distant forests.

It will stalk anything that chances, from street-pigeon to sparrow, but it is chiefly the rodents—the rats and mice—swarming in our cities that it hunts. And it is no exaggeration to say that in this context it plays a highly important part in the balance of nature in urban areas, for it is the most numerous and most active predator there. Without these millions of feral cats, the problem of rats and mice would be even more serious than it is. Man by his wastefulness and uncleanly ways contributes greatly to the rodent menace; by his callousness he has, to some degree, helped to find an answer, however limited.

Ironically, one of the useful jobs the feral cat may perform in various English towns is to check the colonies of hamsters that are developing as a result of escapes. Once upon a time, the golden hamster, native of Western Europe and Syria, was top of the pops on the pet-charts; maybe it, too, will graduate to being a feral species.

CHAPTER TEN

Shadows of the Past

Of the large mammals, only the deer still occasionally strays within the city gates to remind us of the days when town and country merged more easily together. The deer that adorn municipal parks all over the world are only half-wild, but they are nevertheless welcome links with nature.

Some years ago when I was in Stockholm, an enormous traffic jam built up one evening rush hour, all the more frustrating because for long it was unexplained. It turned out that the chaos had been caused by a little herd of elk straying in from the forests on the edge of the suburbs. Becoming increasingly confused, they had wandered deeper into the city streets. Eventually forest wardens and police had rounded them up and turned them back into the countryside, thousands of home-going Swedes being late for their smorgasbord that evening. Those stately, massive deer were a bizarre sight—nature had really invaded the city, just as in Canada and America, the beautiful, swift-running white-tailed deer sometimes wanders into town—occasionally in the past as far as the Bronx area of New York, for example.

Of course that scene in Stockholm was not often to be expected in an urban area, let alone a bustling city. It was a reflection of the way the elk population in Sweden has increased, there now being an estimated 300,000. In other parts of Europe there has been a similar increase in the numbers of this magnificent deer, the world's largest, which at times weighs up to 1800 pounds and stands very nearly eight feet at the shoulder (in North America the animal is known as the moose, whereas the American 'elk' is a relation of the red deer).

The antlers of the deer family (carried only by the males except in the case of reindeer in which both sexes wear them) are a unique phenomenon. In the elk or moose they reach their most splendid, and it is hard to credit that these astonishing appendages, with their broad, flattened surfaces and numerous tines, which can attain a span of six feet and a weight of sixty pounds, are grown anew every year, only to be discarded in late winter or spring and give way to fresh and ever larger growth.

In the Moscow region, elk, a protected species in the USSR, frequently wander into the city from the surrounding forests. A typical instance was an elk calf found browsing in a front garden close to a Metro station. Another strayed into the courtyard of a block of flats on the banks of the river Moskva, not very far from Red Square. Both animals were duly carted back to the forest by lorry. In Estonia, the elk population had swelled

In the wild, even if it's in Richmond Park, young mammals born above ground must be quickly mobile, like this week-old red deer fawn. And unlike young mammals such as fox-cub or kitten, it is born with open eyes.

so much and animals so persistently visit towns like Revel, that out of an estimated population of 20,000, 8000 have been culled to keep the numbers under control. Perhaps these town-visiting elk are impelled by what might be called a folk memory of the far-off days before the wild animals were driven out by man.

The nearest truly wild deer close to the English capital are in Epping Forest, now a shadow of its former self and comprising some 6000 acres bought by the City of London to save it from the same fate as that of

The roe deer is more numerous than is sometimes realized, for it is shy and nocturnal, a four-footed shadow. It is far less gregarious than red or fallow deer, living in a family unit, though in winter small parties may come together.

nearby Hainault Forest which was hacked down in Victorian times to make a fortune for some speculator. Ever since the Bronze Age, with ever-increasing rapidity, we have been denuding our country of its trees.

In the days when Epping was part of the hunting preserve of Waltham Abbey (the sporting abbot being as typical of mediaeval times as the sporting squire later on), red deer roamed extensively the glades and brakes that are now covered by suburban semis, television masts rearing up instead of the antlers of the deer. But the remnants of those red deer were removed to Windsor in the early 1800s, while in 1883 roe deer were reintroduced from Dorsetshire by the chief verderer, E. N. Buxton, helped by J. E. Harting, author of the classic *Extinct British Animals*. Part of my childhood was spent in Epping Forest and I can still remember my ecstasy—the only word for it—at the sight—a glimpse—of a family group of roe deer, buck, doe, fawn —which vanished as swiftly as some brief heart-rending scene in a dream. Indeed, I dreamt about those almost fairy-like deer afterwards.

A unique characteristic of the roe and a reliable way of ascertaining their presence, even without sighting them, is their so-called fairy rings round which during the August rut the buck chases the doe interminably until well-worn circles are left. According to an ancient belief in Scotland, these games took place round a 'spaning-tree' when the doe wanted to distract her young one at time for it to be spaned or weaned.

But that conservationist experiment did not last. Half a century after their reintroduction all the roe had vanished. It could be said, without overstretching a point, that in a way the roe's place in that now urban area is being taken by the muntjak. This tiny, foxy-red deer, also known as the barking deer because of its dog-like alarm cry, is a native of south-east Asia, but was brought extensively to Britain to decorate various noble properties, from which it has constantly escaped and is now a feral species.

Nowadays it can almost be said to be colonizing the Epping Forest area, and is an occasional visitor to suburban gardens there, browsing on cherished shrubs and picking up fallen apples. Its small size—it is smaller even than the roe—and elusive ways enable it to remain concealed to an extent probably little realized by the human commuters who, also, have colonized the area. But the genuinely wild cervine denizens of an historic region are the herd of fallow deer that still linger on in Epping. Up to the days of William IV it was said that hundreds of deer could be seen by coach travellers on their way to and from Harwich. Progressively, however, widespread poaching by the notorious 'Waltham Blacks' brought the herd to the verge of extinction and by 1860 only about a dozen remained.

In the nick of time the Reverend J. W. Maitland came to the rescue, the survivors were strictly protected and nowadays perhaps a hundred of the deer remain in spite of the hazards and disturbance caused by thousands of Londoners (and their ubiquitous dogs) who take to the forest as a blessed relief from their suburban existence. But one of the worst dangers to the deer is the traffic along the various roads running out of London through Epping and there are many casualties every year.

Both red and roe are indigenous to Britain, but the fallow, a native of Mediterranean countries, was reputedly introduced by the Romans (along with the pheasant), though in Epping the belief was that the Danes had brought them, an unlikely theory. Whatever the case, the fallow deer of Epping are unique in always having been truly wild, in comparison with the animals that grace many an aristocratic park. Their colour differs greatly, too, the fallow in general being a reddish-fawn dappled with white spots ('fallow' here meaning palish brown or reddish yellow), whereas the Epping deer are all a uniform dark brown which shows up as black, the mottles and spots invisible at any distance. Indeed, locally, the animals used to be called black deer.

In London itself, deer exist in four of the Royal Parks—Greenwich, Hampton Court, Bushy, and Richmond. Greenwich was first stocked early in the reign of Henry VIII by one Eustace Browne, who was paid £13 6s 8d—

a wry commentary on the never-ending downhill slide of money. By the beginning of the present century 150 deer remained; nowadays there are barely a couple of dozen. Hampton Court retains something like 125 fallow deer; Bushy Park 200 fallow and nearly 80 red deer.

But above all it is Richmond Park, with its rolling grassland and stretches of bracken and ancient oak trees—a jewelled enclave in the midst of a polluted jungle of tarmac and concrete—that is most closely associated with town deer. At the time of Queen Victoria's Diamond Jubilee nearly 1200 fallow deer and 50 red deer roamed the park. Nowadays those figures and proportions have changed considerably: there are some 350 fallow deer and 250 red deer. To keep these numbers under control, the deer, property of the Queen, are culled regularly and the venison is sent to fortunate recipients such as the prime minister and the archbishops, while the remainder is sold in Smithfield Market.

Up to the First World War, a number of stags were transferred each year to the royal park at Windsor. Very strong rope nets with meshes ten inches square would be set up across a narrow gap between the woodland and the ponds, with a huge pollard oak tree forming an ambush in which the head keeper and his half-dozen assistants were concealed. A large posse of horsemen would make a sweep through the park and when they had located the herd they would gradually cut out some of the finest stags, which, with the aid of a couple of specially trained deerhounds, would be driven at breakneck speed towards the nets. As soon as one of the stags was enmeshed, down would leap the watching keepers, seize it bodily and bind its feet with leather straps before man-handling it into a waiting vehicle, which was labelled 'Her Majesty's Cart'. The worst indignity the stags suffered was to have the tips of their antlers sawn off to make room for them in the railway wagon they were to travel in.

These 'London' deer are, within obvious limits, completely free, but cannot be regarded as more than semi-wild. Nevertheless, they provide the townsman (who in certain respects is far less free!) with a marvellous chance of being in touch with nature. The melancholy roaring of the stags in the rutting season, the clash of antlers as they spar with one another, the fawns of May and June, are all a fragile redolence of a distant age before man became the prisoner of his own self-made, artificial environment.

W. H. Hudson, that strange, somehow lonely man, who, having been reared on the pampas of the Argentine, then came to England where he lived much of his time in London, although his books about the English countryside are unsurpassed, found great pleasure and much material in the London parks—Clissold Park in Stoke Newington and Hyde Park, where the statue of Rima, the heroine of his novel *Green Mansions*, constitutes the Hudson Memorial. But above all it was Richmond Park he loved and in one of his best-known books, *A Hind in Richmond Park*, he evokes something of this relic of the wild past represented by the deer.

In the autumn these red deer stags will not gather in such amity. They will moan and wallow in the urgency of the rut and their antlers clash angrily.

Nowadays the roe is more numerous than the red deer, yet in the eighteenth and nineteenth centuries it was practically extinct except in the Highlands of Scotland.

Seeing a hind lying under an oak tree, chewing the cud, I drew quietly towards her and sat down at the roots of another tree about twenty yards from her. She was not disturbed at my approach, and as soon as I had settled quietly down the suspended cud-chewing was resumed, and her ears, which had risen up and then were thrown backwards, were directed forwards towards a wood about two hundred yards away. I was directly behind her, so that with her head in a horizontal position and the large ears above the eyes, she could not see me at all. She was not concerned about me—she was wholly occupied with the wood and the sounds that came to her from it, which my less acute hearing failed to catch, although the wind blew from the wood to us.

Undoubtedly the sounds she was listening to were important or interesting to her. On putting my binocular on her so as to bring her within a yard of my vision, I could see that there was a constant succession of small movements which told their tale—a sudden suspension of the cud-chewing, a stiffening of the forward-pointing ears, or a slight change in their direction; little tremors that passed over the whole body, alternately lifting and depressing the hairs of the back—which all went to show that she was experiencing a continual succession of little thrills. And the sounds that caused them were no doubt just those which we may hear any summer day in any thick wood with an undergrowth—the snapping of a twig, the rustle of leaves, the pink-pink of a startled chaffinch, the chuckle of a blackbird, or sharp little quivering alarm-notes of robin or wren, and twenty besides . . .

The sounds that held her attention were inaudible to me, but I dare say that a primitive man or pure savage who had existed all his life in a state of nature in a woodland district would have been able to hear them, although not so well as the hind on account of the difference in the structure of the outer ear in the two species. But what significance could these same little woodland sounds have in the life of this creature in its present guarded, semi-domestic condition—the condition in which the herd has existed for generations? It is nothing but a survival—the perpetual alertness and acute senses of the wild animal, which are no longer necessary, but are still active and shining, not dimmed or rusted or obsolete as in our domestic cattle, which have been guarded by man since Neolithic times.

Nature remains true to herself, even in the city, and Hudson's London hind is an example of how sometimes, albeit only tenuously, the townsman can recreate himself by contact with the wild, even the ghosts of the wild.

The original purpose of the deer herds in what are now parks within London's boundaries was for the royal pleasure—the pleasure of the chase—

> The chase, the sport of kings;
> Image of war, without its guilt

—for who could expect a feeling of guilt to stir within the hunter's breast!

Hyde Park, for example, was a favourite hunting ground of Henry VIII, while in the reign of James I foreign ambassadors enjoyed the privilege of hunting there with bow and hounds. Poaching was rife and many a wretch from nearby London was hanged for his crimes at Hyde Park Gate. As with so many estates all over England, the Civil Wars caused the break-up, or more likely the slaughter of the deer herd, but at the Restoration Charles II introduced a new herd and the last royal hunt in Hyde Park took place during the reign of George III.

Nowadays Hyde Park comprises 340 acres, but even supposing that in bygone days it was larger, hunting so close to the ever-sprawling capital could never have been so wide-ranging as in, say, the New Forest, that ancient royal domain. But at least it was not as brutal as some of the affairs that went on in French or German royal parks which subsequently became town parks and open spaces. By means of enormous canvas screens, twelve feet high, a killing-ground was laid out, the deer were gradually rounded up and driven into it, whereupon the gallant and royal sportsmen would move in and begin the slaughter, applauded by their ladies installed in specially erected stands and regaled by suitable music.

However, some of these sporting princes shared their fun with the hoi-polloi. At one of these massacres an eighteenth-century diarist noted that ten thousand spectators from the neighbouring town gathered on the nearby slopes to witness the royal hunt.

A red deer scrounging food from a motorist in Richmond Park may not be nature at its wildest, but at least it's preferable to that.

The muntjac is most widespread in counties such as Bedfordshire, Buckinghamshire and Hertfordshire, but it shows signs of spreading into other areas.

In Milton's words—
Sweet the coming on
Of grateful evening mild then silent night—
in this case on Wimbledon Common close to the centre of London.

CHAPTER ELEVEN
Living Waters

Every city pond teems with plant and animal organisms, rich in interest for the microscopist. For example, in the lakes of New York's Central Park it has been calculated that three trillion of such living forms exist. But most townsfolk are more aware of the fish and birds in city waters.

One of the pictures evoked by mentioning fish in city rivers is of single-minded optimists sitting on the *quais* of Paris, their floats bobbing tantalizingly, not because of any roach or gudgeon or miller's thumb taking the bait, but because of the wash of *peniche* or *bateau-mouche* fussing up and down the Seine. Fortunately for these anglers they are comforted by their *pinard*, while it goes without saying that the sun is shining and the 'candles' of the chestnuts have been lit. Otherwise the outlook would be bleak, for, alas, the chances of a bite are nowadays remote. The Seine has been polluted with sewage and factory effluent for several years—yet up to the time of the French Revolution drinking water for Paris was taken direct from the river, while not all that long ago more than sixty species of fish could be caught below the city of Rouen.

Less apparent than bird or beast, fish have suffered at the hands of man to a lamentable degree in rivers and lakes all over the world—Rhine, Rhone, Zurich, Erie, to name but a few. In the Soviet Union alone, nearly a quarter of a million miles of river are seriously polluted, and any fish venturing into urban areas are likely to be asphyxiated through lack of oxygen.

Desperate if belated efforts are being made to amend all this, in some cases with gratifying results. The Thames is by far the most successful instance. Once upon a time Edmund Spenser could apostrophize it as 'Sweet Thames!'—William Morris could dream of 'London, small and white and clean, The clear Thames bordered by its gardens green'—and there used to be a yarn to the effect that salmon were so common in the river that London apprentices stipulated in their articles that they shouldn't be fed on salmon more than twice a week. A pretty tale without any evidence to support it. Nevertheless, salmon were undoubtedly prolific—as late as 1810, Thames fishermen caught three thousand of them in a good year, and later on, in the days of George IV, the artist John Gould watched salmon leaping the weir in the royal town of Windsor: a pity he never painted this, for the returning salmon is a glorious sight, a bar of iridescent silver in the spray, leaping time after time if necessary, higher and higher,

Nature is full of contradictions, exemplified here by this magnificent polar bear,
a mammal that can weigh 1500 pounds and stand five feet at the shoulder,
trying its luck at a rubbish-dump.

Nothing is wasted by nature—not even human ordures, as shown in this picture
of excited birds going to work in their hundreds at a rubbish-tip in Florida.

Milton again—
Towered cities please us then,
And the busy hum of men—
but not these red deer in Richmond Park, which are oblivious to it all.

So keen are people to encourage birds to their homes that artificial nests for
house-martins can be bought. Luckily here, the birds have found plenty of mud.
The martin is very sociable and there was one instance of forty-six nests being
built alongside each other on a nine-yard length of wall.

ten or eleven feet, obeying the irresistible urge to return to its native headwaters and perpetuate its race. The Romans had every reason to call it 'Salar', the Leaper. In a number of towns, such as Romsey in Hampshire on the river Test, and North Tawton on the river Taw in Devonshire, this yearly marvel of nature can still be watched.

But on the Thames the decline had already set in before Gould's time. The naturalist Thomas Pennant, friend and correspondent of Gilbert White, had mentioned before the end of the eighteenth century that Thames salmon were selling at a 'vast price', sure indication of their growing scarcity—and some years later one was sold to the royal household at a guinea a pound, prodigiously dear for those days. It is not known for certain when the last salmon was caught in the Thames, but according to William Yarrell it was in 1833, three years before the publication of his book, *History of British Fishes*.

Many factors contributed to the stifling of the Thames. Gaslight had been introduced to London in 1807, and for the rest of the century gas-works (together with other industrial enterprises) spewed out poisonous effluent. At the same time water closets were becoming fashionable in middle-class homes, to which were added the cesspools 'fed' by working-class privies. Contributions from all of which went towards 'the liquid 'istory' the Thames was claimed by John Burns to comprise. 'Every drop of it.'

The situation went from one climax to another. 1856 was 'The Year of the Great Stink' when, according to *The Times*, parliamentary sessions were abandoned in the greatest haste and confusion because of the stench rising from the Thames, MPs fleeing precipitately, led by the Chancellor of the Exchequer 'who, with a mass of papers in one hand and with his handkerchief clutched in the other and closely applied to his nose, with body half-bent, hastened in dismay from the pestilential odour'. Only when screens soaked in disinfectant were hung from the windows were the parliamentarians able to regain their seats. Again, in 1878, when the paddle-steamer *Princess Alice* was rammed by the *Bywell Castle*, 650 trippers were drowned or, more precisely, mostly asphyxiated by the poisonous quality of the water in which not even the strongest swimmer could survive.

But, relatively speaking, the worst situation developed after the Second World War. War damage to sewers and treatment works—vastly increased industrialization resulting in enormous masses of detergent big enough to overwhelm rivercraft at their moorings—effluent from paper manufacturing plants and many other factories—all deprived the river of its life-giving oxygen.

By 1957 the Thames was a dead river. Not a fish existed in the forty miles between Richmond and Tilbury.

Yet, less than twenty years later it could with truth be claimed that

T. S. Eliot called the river 'a strong brown god'. Strong it certainly was, but a pretty dirty brown in the days sixty years ago when William Wyllie painted this evocative scene of the Thames at Southwark Bridge.

'the restoration of London's river and re-establishment of its wildlife is a feat of unsurpassed credit which at the time it was achieved was unique for its scale in the world'.*

This radical and welcome transformation was not due to any natural miracle. It came about through a change in attitude—in other words, people had raised another Great Stink, metaphorical but positive. This went together with better scientific understanding of pollution problems and the modernization and rationalization of sewage works serving London. Before the last war nearly two hundred of these existed, of dubious efficiency; by 1970 there were only twelve main regional works, all equipped with the most modern filtration, treatment and aeration devices, the resulting fluid discharged into the river being to all intents and purposes pure water, testified to in the BBC's *Panorama* programme by Richard Dimbleby drinking a glassful. In addition, industrial and marine activities were far more strictly controlled by bodies such as the Port of London Authority and the Thames Water Authority.

And the fish came back. Already isolated salmon have been caught in the Inner Thames, one being seen leaping as far up-river as Shepperton Weir, and future restocking of the river is a practical hope. Trout, both brown and rainbow, have become increasingly common and sea-trout are now found quite regularly below London Bridge.

In *Some Account of London* (1701), Thomas Pennant mentioned, among other fish in the Thames, the Allis shad, the lamprey, the smelt—relation of the salmon—the barbel with its characteristic filaments hanging from its mouth, bleak, which are beautiful and lively little fish darting here and there in large shoals, the roach, chub, eel, flounder. All these and many

*Alwyne Wheeler *The Tidal Thames*, 1979.

more once again pursue their mysterious, watery ways in London's river, from the voracious pike to the fidgety loach—which is credited with the knack of forecasting thunderstorms twenty-four hours beforehand. The rehabilitation of the Thames is one of the most cheering examples of urban renewal and one might possibly, just possibly, reasonably call to mind Richard Franck's words from the seventeenth century when he praised the river as 'bountiful, beautiful, and most illustrious, without precedent because of the excellency and delicacy of her fish'.

Success in the fight against pollution in the Thames is without precedent internationally.

But important though fish are, and gratifying their return, people, apart from fishermen, are more likely to be aware of the presence or absence of birds on urban waters. As far as a 'big city' river is concerned, in this case the Thames again, the plight of the birds was comparable with that of the fish. One of the ironies to do with the pollution of the Thames was that the main food supply of the wildfowl was never adversely affected. Indeed, it actually flourished in polluted waters: this was various forms of Tubifex worm, but during the worst of the pollution the birds could not get at these without stirring up the noxious hydrogen sulphide in the mud in which the worms live. By the end of the 1950s, the bird life of the London area of the Thames was confined to a few mallard and mute swans, which depended almost completely on grain spilled from the riverside wharves.

The transformation was as dramatic as in the case of the fish. In a single decade the London reaches of the Thames once again harboured many species of water birds, including a wintering population of around ten thousand wildfowl and twelve thousand waders. Once again, for example, pochard come to the Thames in considerable numbers, flocks of four thousand having been sighted in the London area. The winter population of tufted duck outnumbers even that of mallard; wigeon and teal are regular visitors, while once-scarce birds such as shelduck, pintail and scaup are all coming back to the river. As for waders, one notable beneficiary from the anti-pollution campaign is the oyster-catcher—that handsome pied bird with the long, orange bill and pink legs and sweet, evocative, ringing cry—which has bred in the city area for the first time.

Flocks of lapwing regularly frequent the Thames; ringed plover breed occasionally. Dunlin sometimes appear in large numbers, one year's count in the neighbourhood of Thurrock being put at seven thousand. Redshank, curlew, knot, snipe, ruff, have all been recorded in varying numbers, to-gether with more occasional visitors such as whimbrel, black-tailed godwit, greenshank, grey and golden plover, sanderling, the different sandpipers, and even the avocet and little stint, that diminutive 'globe-spanner' which breeds in the Arctic and winters in Africa.

For once, man has made amends, even in a limited way, and the wild creatures have taken advantage of this, for nature's bush-telegraph seems to work faster than many a man-made communications system.

A striking example of nature's opportunism is in the case of reservoirs. Among the human population for whose benefit these reservoirs are built, there is frequent controversy, either because hitherto unspoilt countryside is threatened or much-needed farmland requisitioned—though water is, to say the least, quite as important as food. Man cannot live by bread alone, as we might say!

No such inhibitions deterred the wild birds. From the start, in the last century, when reservoirs began to replace the haphazard water supplies of cities such as London and New York, they came flocking joyfully to these artificial lakes, many of them in urban areas, in ever-increasing numbers, both for shelter and for food, the latter in various forms, including fish, molluscs, worms, insect larvae, algae, water-plants and all the other natural life that was soon established. Yet it was not until many years had passed that ornithologists began to catch up on the phenomenon. Of course, in those days bird-watchers were far less thick on the ground, unlike nowadays when they often outnumber a rare species, such as the river warbler, in pursuit of which hundreds of 'twitchers' trampled down such an acreage of rye that a fund was raised by conscience-stricken ornithologists to compensate the farmer on whose land the wretched migrant had been reported.

It is interesting to mention how similar were the reactions in Britain and America when, in the early years of this century, ornithologists did begin to appreciate what rich avian treasure the reservoirs were attracting. In *The Naturalist on the Thames*, C. J. Cornish described how at the Barn Elm Reservoirs, between Hammersmith and Putney Bridges, 'the scene over the lakes was as sub-arctic and lacustrine as on any Finland pool, for the frost-fog hung over river and reservoirs, only just disclosing the long, flat lines of embankment water, and ice; the barges floating down with the tide were powdered with frost and snow-flakes, and the only colour was the long, red smear across the ice of the western reservoir, beyond which the winter sun was setting into a bank of snow clouds. It was four o'clock and nothing apparently was moving, either on the ice or the water, not even a gull. In the centre of the north-eastern reservoir was what was apparently an acre of heaped-up snow. On approaching nearer this acre of snow changed into a solid mass of gulls, all preparing to go to sleep. If there was one there were seven hundred, all packed together for warmth on the ice. Beyond the gulls, which rose and circled high above in the fog with infinite clamour, were a number of black objects, which soon resolved themselves into the forms of duck and other fowl. Rather more than seventy were counted, swimming on the water near the bank or sitting on the ice. The result of a look through the glasses was something of a surprise. They were not mallard, teal, or widgeon; but three-quarters of them were tufted

One can't help feeling that in this eighteenth-century picture by T. & W. Daniell of the Jumna at the holy city of Benares (nowadays Varanasi), the ghat has been tidied up for the occasion and many of its winged scavengers banished.

ducks, remarkable proof of the tendency of wild-fowl to increase in this country. When approached, the whole flock rose at once and flew with arrow-like speed round the lakes, but as several birds had not risen, we ventured still nearer, and saw that most of these were coots, some ten or eleven, which did not fly, but ran out on to the ice. Two large birds remaining, which had dived, then rose to the surface, and to our surprise and pleasure proved to be great crested grebes.'

And John Kieran, in the same period, described in *A Natural History of New York City* how thrilled he was to discover that the new reservoirs had been adopted as feeding areas and refuges by many kinds of ducks, gulls, and other waterfowl, including several rare birds. 'I saw them first from the rear window of the attic room in which I slept. I immediately armed myself with field glasses and went out to inspect the ducks at closer range by peering at them through the iron picket fence surrounding the reservoir (the Jerome Reservoir in the Bronx). I remember that the first bird I brought into focus turned out to be a White-winged Scoter and, looking back, I recall seeing Canvasback, Redheads, Goldeneyes, Common Mergansers, and, in all, fourteen different species of waterfowl on the reservoir that winter.'

So sensational was his news at that time, that not only did it feature in the New York *Daily Mail*, but it caused experts from the American Museum of Natural History to rush to the scene to confirm Kieran's exciting discovery!

Progressively since those days not only have more reservoirs been built but vastly increasing numbers of wild birds have taken to using them— partly because this has coincided with the equally progressive disappearance of many of the 'wetlands' once frequented by such birds. In the London area, for example, Cornish's 'seven hundred gulls' have turned into a quarter of a million and more—common, herring, greater and lesser black-backed, but chiefly the black-headed gull, roosting on the waters. On the Queen Elizabeth II reservoir alone, one hundred thousand have been regular visitors. Other less well-known species such as the kittiwake, little-gull, even the glaucous and Iceland gulls, have been seen, as well as black and common and Arctic terns, with their beautiful, tapered bodies that look like porcelain and their delicate, fluttering wings—which contrast with their scolding, skirring cries and often aggressive behaviour.

As for Cornish's pleasure and surprise at spotting that pair of great crested grebes, he would have been gratified to know that few winters pass without red-backed, black-necked, and Slavonian grebes being recorded, while from time to time spectacular visitors such as the red-throated and great northern divers have been seen, their wild wailing redolent of their distant Arctic homes.

And what of those seventy tufted duck—the 'magpie-diver' as it used to be called by wildfowlers?

In one winter alone on the very small Stoke Newington reservoirs, four miles from the centre of London, two thousand were counted, while other species have included shoveller, goldeneye, smew, goosander, red-breasted merganser—not to mention the mallard, teal, and widgeon, of which even Cornish spoke dismissively.

These urban reservoirs have become so important, especially as wintering grounds for so many migratory wildfowl, that an International Wildfowl count is held on them every year. Reservoirs are regarded by ornithologists as among the most rewarding places for bird-watching, while through their comparative proximity to city areas, they provide the townsman with a marvellous opportunity of being in touch with nature, particularly as so many of the species have winged their secret way long distances from the far north.

The reservoirs created an entirely new habitat for many wild birds, man for once acting as a creator instead of destroyer. But this was merely fortuitous. He certainly didn't have the waterfowl in mind when building those huge artificial lakes. All that concerned him was an adequate water-supply for the growing millions in his cities. In London, for example, until the reign of Queen Victoria, one water company at Chelsea was taking supplies direct from the Thames immediately alongside the outflow from a large sewer. In Paris at the time of Louis-Philippe (brought to power in the revolution of 1830) there was a pumping station by the Pont Notre Dame drawing water from the river Seine into which a hellish brew of ordures was regularly deposited. In New York at the same period many townsfolk depended on rainwater collected from the roofs, while other water was brought in from outlying districts and sold on the streets.

But when man built his ornamental lakes in park and on common, he *did* have the birds in mind. This implicit yearning for the company of nature is one of the ironies of our make-up. We have destroyed so much wildlife, yet at the same time we hanker for living reminders of the animal kingdom to which we belong—hence, for example, our establishment of zoos through the ages, from the days of the ancient Chinese or Queen Hatshepsut. And hence our pleasure in stocking our ornamental ponds with wildfowl.

Such city lakes exist worldwide, from the Bois de Boulogne to the parks of Rest and Culture in Moscow, but one of the best-known and most noted for its wild bird population is London's St James's Park, inaugurated by James I early in the seventeenth century. He was greatly interested in 'outlandish fowl' and his collection became, in the words of John Evelyn (that highly interesting diarist overshadowed by his more racy contemporary, Samuel Pepys), 'a singular and diverting thing, stored with numerous flocks of several sorts of ordinary and extraordinary wild fowle'.

Some of the waterfowl there have indeed been both outlandish and extraordinary, having included such unlikely characters as golden eagles brought from the highlands of Scotland and cormorants from the Farne Islands, the title of the warden of the collection in Charles II's days being Keeper of Hawks and Cormorants. But the most bizarre specimens to have been plonked down on a metropolitan lake have been various North American pelicans, some of them sent by a friendly Governor of Louisiana (where Audubon had once come across several hundred, perched on the mangrove trees, 'seated in comfortable harmony, as near each other as the strength of the branches would allow').

Unfortunately, the St James's Park pelicans, whatever their interest to the public, made themselves unpopular with the authorities by a regrettable tendency to tuck unwary ducklings into their well-known pouches. The mute swans, too, also became extremely hostile to the pelicans, no doubt fearing for their cygnets—and an angry swan is a formidable creature, its magnificent wings quite capable of breaking a man's leg or ending the career of the venturesome dog.

Though many unusual water birds have been kept on such ornamental lakes, from the black swan of Australia to the Abyssinian blue-winged

Water, flowing or still, is always one of the richest gathering places of wildlife, affording the city birdwatcher an endless source of pleasure. This picture is of the Eagle pond at Snaresbrook in Epping Forest.

goose, it is in general the various species of wild duck that are the most numerous, including the most familiar such as mallard and teal and widgeon and those less well-known to the town-dweller such as the shoveller and the ruddy shelduck, the gadwall and the garganey and many others. Most of these specimens are pinioned; even so they provide not only pleasure and colour, but also an excellent means of practising one's powers of identification—helped by the illustrated tiles put up in many parks. Many an ornithologist has been fired originally by such opportunities.

In addition, these pinioned birds, acting as unwitting and innocent decoys, attract genuinely wild members of their own species, while other separate wild birds such as coot and moorhen and dabchick enjoy the shelter—and free food!—these ornamental aquatic pleasaunces provide. Even the majestic heron has nested in Hyde Park, no doubt with an eye to the sticklebacks and roach and gudgeon in the Serpentine, while once upon

a time a large heronry existed in the Sidmouth Plantation of Richmond Park, fifty or sixty birds being recorded occasionally.

As for the kingfisher, that wonder of a bird that seems to live in a blaze of celestial fire, Hudson stated surprisingly that it was a frequent visitor to the London parks, drawn by the abundance of small fish in the ornamental waters and the boskage provided by the wooded islands. Reminiscent of Charles Waterton's successful encouragement of sand-martins by building a cliff for them to nest in, he suggested constructing a special rockery with nesting holes on one of the islets—such nests would soon have been turned into malodorous sumps through the remains of all the small fry and tadpoles and aquatic insects kingfishers take to their young. Nowadays the kingfisher is virtually unknown in the London area, except in the wilder parts of Bushy Park, for example, where it has been known to breed in recent years.

But it does penetrate urban areas. In my local town of Figeac in southwest France I once watched no fewer than a dozen kingfishers operating from a weir on the river Célé, oblivious to the noise and bustle of the market and the constant thunder of traffic, including international lorries, along the embankment. Scarcely bigger than a sparrow, if you discount that long beak, the kingfisher is one of the most spectacular birds, with its jewelled, arrowlike, headlong flight, its fairy-tale colours of dark emerald and cobalt and ruddy chestnut, and its skilful, darting plunge from a favourite fishing-perch.

One kingfisher is a precious enough experience; the sight of that little *flock* was almost unreal—like some extravagant illustration by an Edmund Dulac! Probably it comprised two families which had been driven farther down-stream by the drought that was progressively drying up their shallower haunts. What would Dame Alice Berners' collective noun be for them— a charm of goldfinches, an exalting of larks—perhaps a lustre of kingfishers?

The nearest heronries to the centre of London are at Walthamstow reservoirs and Kempton Park. But nationwide the numbers of herons have progressively diminished during recent years, partly through the destruction of habitat.

Wild flowers and ferns conceal the scars of war.

CHAPTER TWELVE
Nature and Man

The war damage, spoliation and industrial waste mentioned in this last chapter epitomize how nature never misses a chance to fill that vacuum she traditionally abhors. For the city-dweller who cares to look and to seek, wildlife in one form or another abounds on all sides—the amoeba in the local pond—the ants going their sedulous way on the footpath—the shepherd's purse and the timothy and the numberless other wildflowers that steal in—the fox that regards the local common as his province. Provided we do not eventually turn the earth into a barren moonscape, nature will always be with us, often in spite of us and often without our knowledge.

Even where man destroys or abandons, nature takes immediate advantage. The classic case in this connection is the blitz of London during the 1939–45 war, when hundreds of thousands of buildings were destroyed or badly damaged. On the bomb-sites in the metropolis (and of course in other blitzed towns) nature moved in at once, as if in her various forms she had been lurking constantly in the air, waiting for such an opportunity. And indeed her seeds were in a way literally doing this, brought all the time on the prevailing westerly winds, but falling mostly on barren ground in areas where the buildings stood shoulder to shoulder, allowing little chance of their taking hold. But when 'the blast of war blew in our ears' and cut a swathe through that concrete huddle, nature slipped in.

Many wild flowers—coltsfoot, ragwort, groundsel, Canadian fleabane, and starry scores of others, took roothold among the ruins left by Hitler's bombers. Undoubtedly the most notable plant colonization was in the case of the densely growing rosebay willow-herb which soon became the commonest wildflower in Central London and helped a little to soften with its lovely rose-pink masses the traces of man's beastliness to man.

And nature, being always logical, sent in with the rosebay willow-herb, the handsome elephant hawk-moth, for the plant is the favourite food of its larvae. It is not fanciful to see the connection between the beautiful, rosy-pink colours of this soft-winged creature and those of the fireweed—as the willow-herb is known in Canada because of its liking for burnt-out patches of forestland. (After the Great Fire of London in 1666, according to the naturalist John Ray, the ruined building plots of the city were covered with rocket, or London rocket, as it became known as a result.)

Altogether something like 125 wild flowers, hitherto unknown in the area, were found to have colonized these bomb-sites, while shrubs or trees

The townsman yearns for contact with nature, even when, by implication, he mocks the animals—though he admits his relationship with them by dressing them up.

such as hawthorn, rowan, elder, bramble, and buddleia all became established, temporarily at least, so that for a time it might have seemed that the letting in of the jungle was taking place and that Kipling's words were being fulfilled.

> Veil them, cover them, wall them round—
> Blossom, and creeper and weed—
> Let us forget the sight and the sound,
> The smell and the touch of the breed!

Inevitably, with the establishment of so much plant life and, needless to say, insect life, providing shelter and food, many birds colonized the bomb-sites. Goldfinches found much seed-food, even some of the warblers such as willow-warbler and whitethroat and blackcap found ideal protection among the rampant growth that had smothered so many of the blackened ruins. House-sparrows, too, profited from the immensely increased nesting space afforded, for that is as important as food itself to the wild creatures. Kestrels weren't slow to notice the increased sparrow population . . .

But the bird most intimately associated with the results of the London blitz was the black redstart. All black in the male except for a white wing-patch and the rufous tail common to all redstarts ('start' deriving from the Anglo-Saxon *steort*, meaning a tail), this smart, migratory relation of the robin had for long been an extremely rare bird in Britain, nesting for the first time sixty years ago, when T. A. Coward, knowing it only as an occasional winter visitor in the south-west, could puzzle over where it came from and describe 'how the little dusky males flicked their fiery tails as they clung to the rocks, hunting for spiders and insects in every crack and crevice'.

How nature's grapevine works must always remain a mystery and a wonder. But word got round among the black redstarts of southern Europe and north Africa that the bomb-sites of London offered not only a plentiful insect supply but also unlimited nesting sites in the holes and crannies of the ruined buildings—which in addition were admirably free from human interference. Some birds even took to wintering in the charred city.

Gradually, however, as the bomb-sites were cleared and monstrous buildings climbed into the sky again, the black redstart was deprived of much of its new-found habitat and its numbers consequently diminished once more. But its thin, pleasant, tentative, robinlike song continues to be heard in some parts of east London, such as the Tower Hamlets area.

Nature has taken advantage not only of man's wilful destruction in the shape of war damage, but where he has simply abandoned some project or other—ravaging the earth then moving on to a fresh area, just as, for different purposes, his neolithic ancestors once did, and as certain primitive people still do in parts of the world.

Even the slag heaps that tower over many mining towns are important storehouses of rare fossil remains of plants, fish, insects, amphibia, but as far as living wildlife is concerned, abandoned gravel pits are rich new habitats created out of man's waste. Modern construction works, motorways, roads, houses, factories, airports, require enormous quantities of gravel and sand, for example, with the result that parts of the country have been pock-marked with these pits and quarries, many of them in urban areas.

As soon as they are exhausted and man abandons them, nature moves in. Before long the pits fill with water, itself one of the great natural bases of life. Bulrushes, flowering sedges, rushes, reed-mace, and many other

An abandoned gravel-pit can be a veritable laboratory for the naturalist, embracing many aspects of nature—bird-life, plant-life, small mammals, fish, insects, amphibians.

larger plant species too numerous to catalogue, find roothold, followed by larger plants such as willows and sallows. At the same time aquatic insects, from dragonfly to water-boatman, appear, too, followed by frog and toad and newt, all grateful for this new habitat—especially as they have suffered from the land drainage that has deprived them of many of their former haunts.

The birds are not far behind. Many an abandoned sand-pit has been immediately colonized by sand-martins, while in the case of gravel-pits, the bird life is probably as varied as on many reservoirs, even though less numerous. Mute swan and dabchick, reed-warbler and great crested grebe, mallard, coot, moorhen—with these and so many other examples of wildlife, apparently insignificant disused gravel-pits on the outskirts of many towns provide a constant source of enjoyment for the local ornithologist and naturalist.

Probably the most interesting example of an avian species taking advantage of old gravel-pits is the little ringed plover. Before the end of the last war this bird had only once been known to nest in Britain, though it breeds extensively in Holland. Yet nowadays as many as twenty-five pairs have bred every year in abandoned sites, especially in the London area, and its characteristic pip-pip adds a cheerful note as this tiny, chubby, round-headed bird runs, stops, listens with up-raised head, then runs on again in search of minute freshwater crustacean or mollusc.

There is one pleasant case in which both nature and people have taken advantage of the abandonment of a human project. This is the derelict Surrey Docks at Rotherhithe in the East End of London. Abandoned since 1970, this once flourishing scene of commercial activity now provides a three-hundred-acre refuge for an astonishing variety of bird life—red-legged or French partridge, skylark, kestrel, reed bunting, ringed plover, yellow wagtail, greenshank, cuckoo, goldfinch, red-crested pochard, whinchat, goosander, scaup, ferruginous duck, black redstart, heron, greenfinch.

And this jumble of derelict warehouses, mounds of bulldozed earth, drained dock-basins, grassy plains, has become a profitable 'hunting ground' for the East End Wildlife Group, itself an outstanding example of how the townsman can enjoy the astonishing world of nature that constantly dwells, seen or unseen, heard or unheard, within the city gates.

Some years ago Richard Fitter remarked that 'kestrels would be a much commoner sight in the London sky if gazing upwards were not such a dangerous occupation in the traffic-laden streets'.*

In principle that applies to all wildlife in the city, not that it is a question of simply gazing upwards but rather on all sides and down at the earth itself. And though it can't be suggested that urban areas (that bleak term) are coming to resemble a scene by Henri 'le Douanier' Rousseau, with wild eyes peering from the undergrowth, there is a teeming amount of wildlife in city and town and suburb which the townsman is often unaware of or takes for granted or does not pause to consider it because it seems too insignificant.

Quite evidently it has not been the purpose of this book to catalogue all the species that have been recorded in the 'city'; that would have been neither possible nor desirable. This isn't a check-list or a handbook. There is no lack of worthy guides on that score. But from V-shaped wedges of Canada geese honking their romantic way high above the skyscrapers of New York, to the fierce dytiscus water-beetle preying on the tadpoles in a suburban pond—from a ruby-throated hummingbird in an Ontario garden to a holly blue on Wimbledon Common, from big-tooth aspen to mugwort, nature in one form or another lives side by side with us, a fact surely to be welcomed.

For to use the words of Hayo Hoekstra in *Naturopa*, 'Could we exist shut up in our towns, as we are most of the time, unless we had some

---

*London's Natural History, 1945.

We must call in nature to transform our urban deserts into green oases.

Shepherding this wild duck and her brood to safety in St James's Park is surely a
contradiction of W. S. Gilbert's claim that
When constabulary duty's to be done,
The policeman's lot is not a happy one.

Symbolic of a rare but ideal partnership—the splendour of man-made St Paul's
and the ineffable beauty of nature.

contact with nature? Is it possible for man to conceive a balanced and
happy life that does not obey the laws of nature? Is it right for us to live,
as individuals, nations and races, by offending and mutilating nature and
causing animal and plant species to vanish forever from the face of the
earth?'

Our cities and large towns are shrinking in human numbers. The
population of London, for example, is at its lowest this century. If we had
the will we could transform many derelict inner city areas—those gaunt,
satanic, abandoned warehouses, those miles of soulless, unimaginative
streets that breed violence as abundantly as they do bed-bugs—into
oases which nature could colonize and beautify. And at the same time as
we benefited nature—which is so hard-pressed everywhere—we could help
to refresh ourselves, in the same way as the giant Antaeus who, when he felt
his strength ebbing, renewed himself again by stooping down to touch the
earth once more and thereby being restored.

References

Buxton, E. N., *Epping Forest*, London, 1898
Buxton, John A., *The Naturalist in London*, London, 1974
Collenette, C. L., *A History of Richmond Park*, London, 1937
Cornish, C. J., *The Naturalist on the Thames*, London, 1902
Coward, T. A., *Bird Haunts & Nature Memories*, London, 1922
Dagg, Anne Innis, *Canadian Wildlife & Man*, Toronto, 1974
Dorst, J., *Avant que Nature meure*, Neuchatel, 1965
Fabre, J. H., *Souvenirs Entomologiques*, Paris, 1879
Fitter, R., *London's Natural History*, London, 1945
Harrison, J. & Grant, P., *The Thames Transformed*, London, 1976
Hudson, W. H., *Birds in London*, London, 1898
     A Hind in Richmond Park, London, 1922
Jefferies, R., *Nature near London*, London, 1893
Kieran, J., *A Natural History of New York City*, Boston, 1959
Lancum, H., *Wild Birds & Wild Mammals & the Land*, London, 1948/51
London Natural History Society, *The Birds of London since 1900*, London, 1957
Pennant, T., *Some Account of London*, London, 1701
Rublowsky, J., *Nature in the City*, New York, 1967
Simms, E., *Wild Life in the Royal Parks*, London, 1974
     The Public Life of the Street Pigeon, London, 1979
Summers-Smith, D., *The House Sparrow*, London, 1963
Wheeler, A., *The Tidal Thames*, London, 1979
Wilson, F. P., *The Plague in Shakespeare's London*, Oxford, 1927
Zinsser, H., *Rats, Lice & History*, London, 1935

Australian National Parks & Wildlife Service
Brisbane Wildlife Survey
Canadian Wildlife Service
City of London Health Department
East End Wildlife Group
London Natural History Society
Ministry of Agriculture Pest Infestation Control
Naturopa
Thames Water
United States Fish & Wildlife Service

Thanks are due for permission to quote the lines from 'Letting in the Jungle' in *The Second Jungle Book* by Rudyard Kipling, published by Macmillan Publishers, Essex Street, London, and details about mice living in cold storage from the New Naturalist *British Mammals* by Dr L. Harrison Matthews, published by William Collins Sons & Co. Ltd of London.

Index

Acknowledgements

The author and publishers would like to thank the following for supplying illustrations:

Colour

Heather Angel 22 (below), 102; Aquila Photographics 55 (below); Ardea 55 (above), 135 (above); Bruce Coleman 22 (above), 103, 135 (below); Jean-Loup Charmet 54; Spectrum Colour Library 23, 134.

Black and white

Heather Angel 45, 47; Aquila Photographics 8, 17, 35, 90, 150; Ardea 11, 36, 59, 85, 86; J. Allan Cash 6, 12, 14, 39, 93, 98/9, 111, 112, 119, 123, 127, 130, 146, 148, 155; Robert Estall 25; Guildhall Library (Godfrey New Photographics) 19, 60/61, 70, 137; Grant Heilman 73; Eric Hosking 33 (below), 40, 72, 76, 120, 144; India Office Library 80, 140; Jacana 33 (above), 44, 89, 124, 128; Frank Lane 43, 107; Linnean Society 29, 66, 75, 79, 84, 115; Nature Photographers 2, 51, 63; Popperfoto 92; Spectrum Colour Library 108; John Topham 16, 26, 31, 65, 71, 83, 93, 96, 105, 132, 143, 152/3, 154.